Lecture Notes in Computer Science   11263

Commenced Publication in 1973
Founding and Former Series Editors:
Gerhard Goos, Juris Hartmanis, and Jan van Leeuwen

More information about this series at http://www.springer.com/series/7410

Andrea Saracino · Paolo Mori (Eds.)

Emerging Technologies for Authorization and Authentication

First International Workshop, ETAA 2018
Barcelona, Spain, September 7, 2018
Proceedings

 Springer

Editors
Andrea Saracino
IIT-CNR
Pisa, Italy

Paolo Mori
IIT-CNR
Pisa, Italy

ISSN 0302-9743 ISSN 1611-3349 (electronic)
Lecture Notes in Computer Science
ISBN 978-3-030-04371-1 ISBN 978-3-030-04372-8 (eBook)
https://doi.org/10.1007/978-3-030-04372-8

Library of Congress Control Number: 2018962143

LNCS Sublibrary: SL4 – Security and Cryptology

Preface

This book contains the papers selected for presentation at the First International Workshop on Emerging Technologies for Authorization and Authentication (ETAA 2018), which was held in Barcelona, Spain, on September 7, 2018, co-located with the 23rd European Symposium on Research in Computer Security (ESORICS 2018).

The workshop program included eight full papers and two short ones concerning the workshop topics, in particular: new techniques for biometric and behavioral-based authentication, authentication and authorization in the IoT and in distributed systems in general, techniques for strengthening password-based authentication and for dissuading malicious users from stolen password reuse, an approach for discovering authentication vulnerabilities in interconnected accounts, and strategies to optimize the access control decision process in the big data scenario.

We would like to express our thanks to the authors who submitted their papers to the first edition of this workshop, thus contributing to making it a successful event. We would like to thank the sponsors of the workshop: the EU Commission-funded projects: Collaborative and Confidential Information Sharing and Analysis for Cyber Protection (**C3ISP**), and European Network for Cyber Security (**NeCS**), Marie Sklodowska-Curie Actions (MSCA), and Innovative Training Networks (ITN). Last but not least, we would like to express our gratitude to the members of the Technical Program Committee for their valuable work in evaluating the submitted papers.

This workshop was supported by the EU Commission-funded projects:

C3ISP: Collaborative and Confidential Information Sharing and Analysis for Cyber Protection. Grant Agreement no. 700294
NeCS: European Network for Cyber Security, Grant Agreement no. 675320

September 2018
Paolo Mori
Andrea Saracino

ETAA Workshop Introduction

IT devices are rapidly becoming more pervasive in several application fields and in everyday life. The major driving factors are the ever-increasing coverage of Internet connectivity, the extreme popularity and capillarity of smartphones, tablets, and wearables, together with the consolidation of the Internet of Things (IoT) paradigm. Indeed, interconnected devices directly control and take decisions on industrial processes, regulate infrastructures and services in smart cities, and manage quality of life and safety in smart homes, taking decisions with user interactions or even autonomously. The involvement of these devices in so many applications unfortunately introduces a set of unavoidable security and safety implications, related to both the criticality of the aforementioned applications and to the privacy of sensitive information produced and exploited in the process. To address these and other related issues, there is an increasing need of instruments to control the access and the right to perform specific actions on devices or data. These instruments must be able to cope with the high complexity of the considered applications and environments, being flexible and adaptable to different contexts and architectures, from centralized to fully distributed ones, able to handle a high amount of information as well as taking into account non-conventional trust assumptions. The considered technologies should regulate the actions of both human users and autonomous devices, being effective in enforcing security policies, still without introducing noticeable overhead, both in terms of performance and user experience. Hence, the design of advanced, secure, and efficient mechanisms for continuous authentication and authorization, requiring limited-to-no active interaction is solicited.

The ETAA workshop aimed at being a forum for researchers and practitioners of security who are active in the field of new technologies for authenticating users and devices, and for enforcing security policies in new and emerging applications related to distributed systems, mobile/wearable devices, and IoT. It aimed to attract original research work covering both theoretical and practical aspects of authentication and authorization.

Paolo Mori
Andrea Saracino

Organization

Workshop Chairs

Paolo Mori   Consiglio Nazionale delle Ricerche, Italy
Andrea Saracino   Consiglio Nazionale delle Ricerche, Italy

Technical Program Committee

Benjamin Aziz	University of Portsmouth, UK
Francesco Buccafurri	Università Mediterranea di Reggio Calabria, Italy
David Chadwick	University of Kent, UK
Gianpiero Costantino	Consiglio Nazionale delle Ricerche, Italy
Gabriele Costa	IMT Lucca, Italy
Francesco Di Cerbo	SAP Lab, France
Carmen Fernandez Gago	University of Malaga, Spain
Vasileios Gkioulos	Norwegian University of Science and Technology, Norway
Jatinder Singh	University of Cambridge, UK
Jens Jensen	Science and Technology Facilities Council, UK
Rossi Kamal	Shanto Mariam University of Creative Technology, Bangladesh
Erisa Karafili	Imperial College London, UK
Georgos Karopulos	JRC, Italy
Hristo Koshutanski	ATOS, Spain
Gabriele Lenzini	University of Luxembourg, Luxembourg
Mirko Manea	HPE Italia, Italy
Charles Morisset	Newcastle University, UK
Silvio Ranise	Fondazione Bruno Kessler, Italy
Francesco Restuccia	Northwestern University Boston, USA
Francesco Santini	Università di Perugia, Italy
Daniele Sgandurra	Royal Holloway, University of London, UK
Debora Stella	Bird & Bird, Italy
Stefano Tranquillini	Chino, Italy
Nicola Zannone	Eindhoven University of Technology, The Netherlands

Contents

Authentication and Authorization Techniques

Authentication and Authorization for Interoperable IoT Architectures

Nikos Fotiou(✉) and George C. Polyzos

Mobile Multimedia Laboratory, Department of Informatics, School of Information Sciences and Technology, Athens University of Economics and Business, Evelpidon 47A, 113 62 Athens, Greece
{fotiou,polyzos}@aueb.gr

Abstract. Advances in technology have enabled the creation of "smart" Things, fostering the vision of the Internet of Things (IoT). Smart Things have connection capabilities, they support Internet protocols and they even come with operating systems and Application Programming Interfaces. The pursuit for a protocol stack that will support the IoT has resulted, so far, in an ecosystem of heterogeneous and non-compatible solutions that satisfy the requirements of particular vertical sectors ("silos"). For this reason, several research initiatives, driven by both academia and industry, investigate the potential of an interoperable IoT architecture, i.e., an architecture that will provide a common and horizontal communication abstraction, which will act as interconnection layer among all prominent IoT protocols and systems. Securing such an architecture, which includes many stakeholders with diverse interests and security requirements, is not a trivial task. In this paper, we present an authentication and authorization solution that facilitates the interoperability of existing IoT systems. This solution achieves endpoint authentication, encryption key establishment, and enables third parties to define fine-grained, domain-specific access control policies. Things store minimal information, perform only ultra-lightweight computations, and are oblivious about the business logic and processes involved in the authentication and authorization procedures. Furthermore, the proposed solution preserves end-user privacy and can be easily incorporated into existing systems.

1 Introduction

Smart Things support a wide range of connectivity options (for example 6LoW-Pan, ZigBee, Bluetooth Low Energy, Ethernet), Inter-networking protocols (like MQTT, CoAP), and even lightweight operating systems (for example RIoT and Contiki). However, the arms race for an "Internet of Things" (IoT) architecture, has resulted in numerous, diverse, and competing systems that often satisfy only the requirements of a particular vertical use case. However, an "interoperable" IoT architecture would provide significant advantages to society (and data producers or owners), allowing (controlled) data use from all domains

© Springer Nature Switzerland AG 2018
A. Saracino and P. Mori (Eds.): ETAA 2018, LNCS 11263, pp. 3–16, 2018.
https://doi.org/10.1007/978-3-030-04372-8_1

by all applications–through silo boundaries.[1] Several research efforts, driven by academia and industry, have sprung up investigating this potential.

Securing smart Things-based systems is a challenging task by itself, therefore it comes as no surprise that the security of an interoperable IoT architecture is a problem that cannot be easily addressed. An interoperable IoT architecture should interconnect various stakeholders with diverse security needs, requirements, and capabilities, it should allow for flexible user identities and generic access control policies, and it should enable federation of security providers while facilitating at the same time compartmentation and isolation of sensitive business processes.

In this paper, we build on our previous work [9] and we present the design, implementation, and evaluation of a security solution that achieves endpoint authentication, encryption key establishment, and access control delegation. The proposed solution, which was tailored to the IoT and is appropriate for constrained devices, enables the interoperability among various stakeholders without sacrificing end-user privacy and security. With our solution, user-related information never leaves user management systems, while service providers can easily secure their offerings.

In this paper we make the following contributions:

- We improve the performance and the security of our original design [9]. In particular with the new design Things do not maintain any state for unauthenticated connections. Furthermore, the new design is compatible with the (D)TLS handshake with pre-shared keys, hence significant security properties can be claimed.
- We extend [9] to support multi-stakeholder IoT-based services, facilitating this way interoperability.
- We implement our solution and we integrate it in the INTER-IoT interoperable gateway [4], enabling its use from all INTER-IoT systems and applications/use-cases.

Even though there are many somewhat similar access control solutions for Internet applications, our solution has been designed for and tailored to the IoT and has many significant advantages in this domain. Furthermore, compared to existing solutions for the IoT, and as discussed later in Sect. 6, our solution is more lightweight, it has better security and privacy properties, it does not require from Things to be online, and completely hides business logic, semantics, and processes from the Things and the end-users. The latter property is of particular importance when it comes to interoperability and business-to-business services. Finally, as we detail in Sect. 3.3, our solution can be integrated into the (D)TLS handshake–(Datagram) Transport Layer Security–hence existing (D)TLS-based applications can benefit from our approach without any modification.

The remainder of this paper is structured as follows. In Sect. 2 we give an overview of our system and we present an illustrative use case. In Sect. 3 we

---

[1] Data (and information) is not only a non-rivalrous good, it is anti-rivalrous [1], providing (potentially) more value the more it is used.

detail the design of our solution and its integration with (D)TLS. In Sect. 4 we evaluate the qualitative and security properties of our solution. In Sect. 5 we discuss the integration of our solution with an existing interoperable IoT platform. We compare our solution with existing related work in Sect. 6 and we provide our conclusions in Sect. 7.

2   System Overview

In order to give a better overview of our system we present the use case of a "smart port" (similar to a use case of the INTER-IoT project [4] not entirely by coincidence). In this use case, illustrated in Fig. 1, port employees want to access resources provided by Things embedded in containers arriving at the port. Container owners want to make sure that these resources can be accessed only by the port employees. On the other hand, the port authority does not want to allow third parties to access its user management system.

Using our solution this problem can be overcome as follows. The port authority extends its user management system to support access control policies, as well as our protocol. Then, it creates an access control policy that defines who are the port employees and assigns to this policy a URI. From a high-level perspective, the user management system of the port authority can now be viewed as an RPC server: whenever a port employee makes a call to the policy URI, using as input call parameters a "token" and his identification data, the server generates and responds back with an encryption key. A policy URI can then be used by container owners to protect their devices (Steps 1–3).

Each container owner "registers" its devices to the user management system of the port authority and receives back a secret key which is installed in the devices, along with the policy URI (steps 4–6). Suppose now that a port employee wants to access some information provided by a protected device. Initially, he sends an "unauthorized request" and receives back a token and the URI of the policy generated during step 1 (steps 7, 8). Then he performs an RPC call to the user management system and obtains an encryption key (steps 9, 10). With our solution, the device can also calculate the same encryption key, offline, without any communication with the user management system. Since both entities, i.e., the port employee and the Thing, now share the same key, they can use it for securely exchanging data using a protocol such as (D)TLS with pre-shared keys (step 11). The encryption key generation process guarantees user authentication and authorization, as well as device authentication.

Our system achieves the following goals:

- **Transparency.** Container owners are oblivious about the implementation, structure, and content of the port authority user management system. The application implemented in the Things, does not contain any port authority specific logic.
- **Flexible security management.** The port authority can modify the access control policy stored in its user management system without needing to update policy URIs or notify container owners.

- **User privacy preservation.** Things learn no user-specific information. They only information they can deduce is that a user has business relationships with a specific user management system.
- **Lightweight security.** Things have to maintain only a secret key and a policy URI per resource. Furthermore, Things do not have to be connected to the Internet, or to any other network.

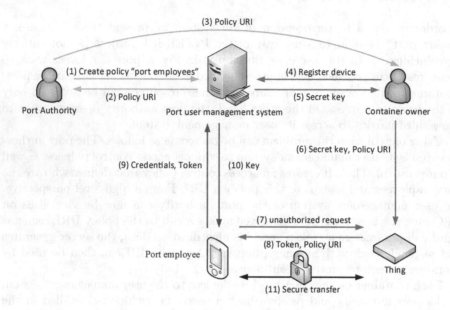

Fig. 1. Smart port use case.

3   System Design

3.1   Preliminaries and Notation

Our construction relies on a keyed-hash message authentication code (HMAC). We refer to the digest of a message m using an HMAC function h and a key k as $h_k(m)$. Moreover, we refer to the concatenation of n messages as $m_1||m_2||...||m_n$. Entities in our system are uniquely identified either by an identifier or a URI. We refer to the identifier of an entity A as ID_A. Similarly, we refer to the URI of entity B as URI_B.

The core entity of our system is the *Access Control Provider* (ACP) (i.e., the "enhanced" user management system of our use case). An ACP implements the following algorithms:

- **storePolicy**(policy): Stores an access control policy and returns a policy unique URI_{policy}.

- **register**(URI_{policy}, $URI_{resource}$): Registers an IoT resource, protected using URI_{policy}, and returns a secret key (sk). This secret key is $URI_{resource}$ specific. An ACP should check if the entity that invokes this algorithm is the legitimate owner of $URI_{resource}$. However, this process is out of the scope of our work.
- **authorize**(identificationData, URI_{policy}, token, $URI_{resource}$): Examines if a user identified by identificationData can be authorized using URI_{policy}. If this is true, it generates a user specific ID_{user} and invokes the keyGen() algorithm described below. The ID_{user} generation process is ACP specific. Every time the same user invokes the *authorize*() algorithm the ID_{user} may be the same (although this enables user tracking): the only requirement imposed by our system is that it must not be possible for two distinct users to receive the same ID_{user}.
- **keyGen**(ID_{user}, URI_{policy}, token): Creates an ephemeral encryption key by calculating $h_{sk}(ID_{user}||URI_{policy}||token)$, where sk is the key generated using the *register* algorithm and *token* is a session specific random number generated by the protected device. It outputs ID_{user} and the ephemeral encryption key.

Each Thing implements the *keyGen*() algorithm as well. Users have some short of business relationship with an ACP. We assume that users can securely communicate with their ACP and ACPs implement a secure method for authenticating users. Finally, users and Things can communicate with each other. We make no security assumption about the latter communication channel, i.e., any third party can monitor and tamper with the messages exchanged between a user and a Thing.

In addition to attackers monitoring the communication channel between users and Things, our threat model assumes unauthorized users trying to get access to a protected resource, as well as malicious devices trying to impersonate legitimate Things.

3.2 Protocols

Our solution is composed of the following protocols: *Setup, Unauthorized request, User authentication and authorization, Authorized request.*

Setup: The goal of the setup protocol is to enable resource owners to "pair" devices that provide a protected resource with one or more ACPs. Every *resource owner* that wants protect a resource $URI_{resource}$ using an access control policy URI_{policy}, invokes over a *secure communication channel* the *register*() algorithm, receives a secret key sk, and installs it in the corresponding Things. It should be noted that resource owners, Things, and end users do not have to be aware about the implementation details and the business semantics and logic of an access control policy: the only information they learn about a policy is its URI_{policy}. A resource owner may register a resource with multiple ACPs. In that case it will configure the Thing with all URI_{policy} and the corresponding secret keys. Furthermore, sks are only used for generating other keys and they are never communicated to other entities.

Unauthorized Request: The goal of the unauthorized request protocol is to provide users with the necessary authentication and authorization information. A user wishing to access a protected $URI_{resource}$ initially sends to the Thing an *unauthorized* request over an unprotected communication channel. Then, the Thing responds with a *token* and a list of URI_{policy}. A token is a public, random variable unique among all sessions of that specific Thing. The protocol used for making these requests is application specific, e.g., a user may request a resource over HTTP, CoAP [15], or any other protocol.

User Authentication and Authorization: With this protocol, users authenticate themselves to an ACP and receive an ephemeral encryption key. Upon receiving a response to an unauthorized request, the user selects a suitable URI_{policy} and invokes the *authorize()* algorithm over a *secure communication channel*. If the user can be authorized for URI_{policy}, the ACP invokes the *keyGen()* algorithm and sends back to the user, the ID_{user} and the ephemeral encryption key, over the same secure communication channel. A Thing can also calculate the same ephemeral key, offline, using the *keyGen()* algorithm. However, no third party, including the user, can calculate this key since the secret key used by the HMAC calculation is only known to the ACP and the Thing. It is reminded that the latter secret key is $URI_{resource}$ specific.

Authorized Request: The goal of this protocol is to enable Things to generate offline the ephemeral key that an authorized user received from the ACP, as well as to provide means for using this key for securing subsequent communication. In order for the Thing to generate the ephemeral key (i.e., invoke the *keyGen()* algorithm) it needs to learn (i) the token it generated during the unauthorized request, (ii) the selected URI_{policy}, and (iii) the ID_{user}. All these can be provided by the user over an unprotected communication channel. Using this key to protect subsequent communication cannot be trivially achieved in a secure way. For this reason, we rely on (D)TLS–although other protocols can be considered as well.

Figure 2 updates Fig. 1 with the defined algorithms, protocols, and entities. The authorized request protocol is not illustrates since for that we consider (D)TLS. In the following we present the integration of our solution with (D)TLS with pre-shared keys.

3.3   (D)TLS Integration

The goal of (D)TLS is to allow two communicating endpoints, a client and a server, to establish a secure communication channel by executing a "handshake" protocol over an unprotected channel [13]. The security of this protocol can

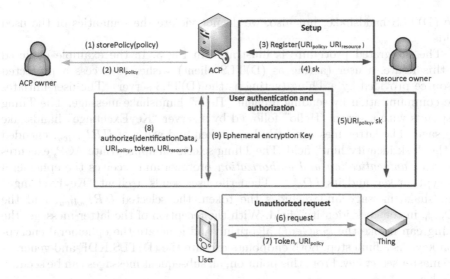

Fig. 2. Algorithms, protocols, and entities of the proposed solution.

be based on public-key cryptography or on a pre-shared secret key [7] (or in a combination of these two approaches). (D)TLS with pre-shared secret key (PSK-(D)TLS) is ideal for constrained devices since it can be implemented using only a few, lightweight operations. With PSK-(D)TLS the communicating endpoints use their pre-shared secret key to derive a "pre-master secret key," and then they use this key as input to a key derivation function (KDF) to calculate a "master secret key". The KDF, in addition to the pre-master secret key, uses as input two random numbers generated by the communicating endpoints and exchanged using the handshake protocol.

In a nutshell (and from a really high perspective), in order to collect the KDF input parameters, a client and a server exchange two "Hello" messages, that include the random numbers selected by each endpoint, and two "KeyExchange" messages that include auxilliary information. Our goal is to use the ephemeral encryption key produced by our solutions as the (D)TLS pre-shared secret key. In particular we implement the unauthorized request and the authorized request protocols using the (D)TLS handshake messages.

The unauthorized request protocol requires from a Thing (server) to send to a user a token and a list of URI_{policy}. This information can be encoded in the "psk_identity_hint" field of the server KeyExchange handshake message. This field is a byte array of size up to 2^{16} bytes and it is used by the server "[...] to help the client in selecting which identity to use." Furthermore, the authorized request requires from a user to send to a Thing the selected URI_{policy}, the generated ID_{user}, and the token. This information can be encoded in the "psk_identity" field of the client KeyExchange handshake message. This field is a byte array of size up to 2^{16} bytes and it is used by the client to " [...] indicate (to the server) which key to use." Hence, not only we can transfer our protocol parameters using the (D)TLS handshake, but also, we do not violate the semantics of the used fields.

The integrated procedure is illustrated in Fig. 3. In the example depicted in this figure, a user (acting as (D)TLS client) wishes to access a protected resource provided by a Thing (acting as the (D)TLS server). The user initiates the communication by sending a client "Hello" handshake message. The Thing responds with a server "Hello" followed by a server "KeyExchange" handshake message. The latter message includes a token and a list of URI_{policy}, encoded in the "psk_identity_hint" field. The Thing selects an appropriate ACP, executes the *user authentication and authorization* protocol and receives the ephemeral encryption key and its ID_{user}. Then the user sends a client "KeyExchange" handshake message and includes the token, the selected URI_{policy}, and the ID_{user} in the "psk_identity" field. With the reception of the latter message, the Thing can invoke the *keyGen()* algorithm and generate the ephemeral encryption key. As a final step, both endpoints execute the (D)TLS KDF and generate the master secret key. From this point on, all subsequent messages can be secured this key.

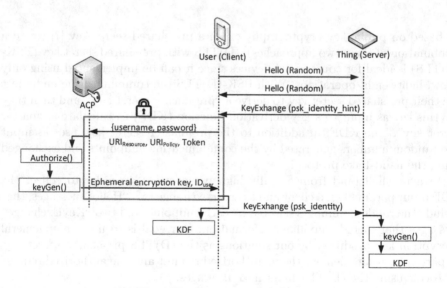

Fig. 3. Integration with (D)TLS.

4 Evaluation

In the following we evaluate our solution. We consider the (D)TLS integrated version. Our solution has the following properties:

It Facilitates Interoperability. Our solution hides the business logic and semantics of each stakeholder. It defines a simple API that allows applications to interact with ACPs and at the same time it gives great flexibility on how an ACP is implemented. ACPs enable compartmentation and isolation of sensitive business processes allowing stakeholders to modify their (security) policies without affecting the applications that are using them. Business-to-Business services can be easily implemented: a company A can offer services to the users of a company B simply by leveraging a URI_{policy} provided by company B.

It Facilitates Application Development. By integrating our solution with (D)TLS we provide a straightforward and transparent way for application developers to include it in their products. As a matter of fact, by incorporating our protocol into the DTLS implementation of the BouncyCastle library[2], and by using a single ACP and hardcoded *identificationData* it was possible to port existing (example) applications without any modification.

It Is Lightweight and It Protects Users' Privacy. With our solution, Things have only to perform a single HMAC calculation, in addition to the operations required by (D)TLS. Furthermore, Things do not have to be connected to the Internet and do not have to maintain any state for unauthorized requests. Finally, Things learn no user specific information apart from the ID_{client}.

4.1 Security Evaluation

Providing that two users (clients) do not share the same pre-shared key and providing that pre-shared keys have enough entropy, PSK-(D)TLS has the following security properties:

- **Communication integrity.** The PSK-(D)TLS handshake protocol makes sure that any modification to the exchanged messages can be detected (but it cannot be prevented).
- **Confidentiality.** The master secret key cannot be guessed and it can be used to protect the integrity and the confidentiality of the messages exchanged after the completion of the handshake.
- **Server authentication.** The PSK-(D)TLS handshake protocol makes sure that man in the middle attacks can be detected (but not prevented). Hence it is not possible for an attacker to impersonate a server.

The pre-shared key used in our solution is the ephemeral encryption key generated by the ACP.

Theorem 1. *Two users identified by different identificationData cannot obtain the same ephemeral key.*

---

[2] https://www.bouncycastle.org/.

Proof. The *keyGen()* algorithm of an ACP, i.e., the algorithm that generates the ephemeral key, uses as input the variable ID_{user}. The latter variable is produced by the *authorize()* algorithm. Given two users identified by *identificationData* A and B respectively, then by definition $authorize(A) \neq authorize(B)$.

PSK-(D)TLS in its simplest form (i.e., without using the Diffie-Hellman key exchange algorithm) does not provide forward secrecy.

An additional security feature of our solution is that it can immediately prevent users with revoked access rights to retrieve a resource. This is achieved by having Things generating a token in every session and by keeping track of the already used tokens: fresh tokens force users to communicate with an ACP in order to retrieve a new ephemeral encryption key. That way, revoked users can be quickly blocked from obtaining such a key.

The security properties of our solution depend on the secrecy of the secret key installed in Things by the resource owners. If this key is breached, then the *setup* protocol should be re-executed for all Things sharing the same key. Nevertheless, no further update is required (e.g., user applications do not have to be modified).

5 Integration with an Existing Interoperable Platform

As proof of concept, we implemented our solution for the INTER-IoT interoperable IoT gateway. INTER-IoT gateway is a modular system that targets to join

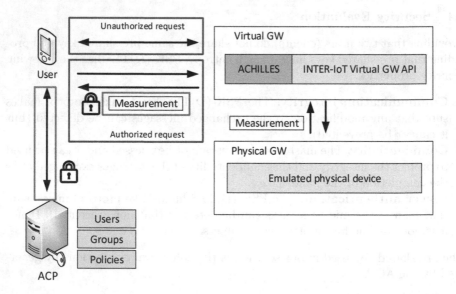

Fig. 4. Integration with the INTER-IoT architecture.

various IoT platforms and technologies under a common API. The INTER-IoT gateway is composed of two parts: the virtual part and the physical part. The physical part provides an abstraction that can be used for interacting seamlessly with Things using various link layer technologies and protocols, whereas the virtual part exposes an API that can be invoked by a user. An API call to the virtual part can be translated into a call to the physical part or it can be translated and forwarded to another IoT platform. If necessary, the user will receive the appropriate response (Fig. 4).

In order to accommodate various technologies, the virtual part of the gateway supports plug-in extensions. We implemented our solution as a plug-in, code-named ACHILLES (stands for Access Control and autHenticatIon deLegation for interoperabLE IoT applications). Our plug-in extends the API of the virtual part of the gateway and implements the protocols described in the previous section.

However, the INTER-IoT API is implemented over HTTP(s), hence our solution had to be implemented at the layer. For this reason, we implemented the TLS KDF in the application layer and we used HTTP headers in order to exchange the necessary information. The derived master secret key is used to encrypt measurements provided by an emulated IoT device. The encrypted measurements are then included in the payload of the HTTP response, sent from the gateway to the user.

As an ACP we used a custom-made user management system. In this system users are identified by a pair of a username and a password. Simple access control policies can be defined using NIST's core Role-based Access Control (core-RBAC) model [8], i.e., the ACP owner creates users, organizes users in groups, and defines access control policies based on these groups. Furthermore, users can communicate with the ACP and exchange data securely using HTTPS.

6   Related Work

The key characteristics of our solution are the following: it is lightweight, it preserves user privacy, it can be used even if Things are not connected to the Internet, Things and applications are business process agnostic, and it is general purpose.

Various systems try to implement Role-Based Access Control (RBAC), or Attribute Based Access Control (ABAC), either by storing user credentials in the Thing or by using a federated identity system, such as OAuth [11] (e.g., as used in [6]) or OpenID [12] (for example, as described in [5]). Storing access control policies in Things raises many scalability and security concerns. For example, updating an access control policy requires communication with all involved Things, whereas with our system, policy modifications take place only on ACPs. Of course, storing user management related information in Things creates many privacy riks. Furthermore, federated identity systems, such as OpenID and OAuth require digital signature verification, which might be too computationally heavy for many IoT devices or applications.

The disadvantages of RBAC/ABAC systems can be overcome by using capabilities tokens. A capabilities token defines the operations that a user is authorized to perform over an object. Capabilities tokens are issued and digitally signed by a third trusted entity. Capabilities-based access control (CBAC) has been studied in the context of the IoT by many research efforts (for example [10, 14]). The main drawback of these systems is that Things have to understand the business logic encoded in a token. With our solution business logic and semantics are transparent to Things and to users.

Eclipse Keti [3] is a token-based access control system which hides business logic from Things. Using Keti, a Thing–or any application–may query an "access control service" if a user is allowed to perform a particular operation. The main drawback of Keti is that it requires Things to be able to communicate with access control services. With our solution Things can be isolated from the rest of the world. Furthermore, using Keti, access control services should be aware of the possible operations that can be executed in a Thing. This creates scalability and privacy issues. Using our system, ACPs (i.e., the entity that holds the same role as the access control service) does not learn the operations that a user wants to perform; it is even possible to hide from an ACP the fact that a user interacts with a Thing. Finally, with our system it is possible to create re-usable policies. For example, the policy "port employees" defined in our use case in Sect. 2 can be used by many systems (not necessarily IoT specific).

Musquitto auth-plug [2] is a plug-in used for authorizing Musquitto MQTT broker users. Musquitto auth-plug can be configured to work with multiple and diverse user management systems and, similarly to our solution, it can be used as a security add-on to an existing deployment. However, this plug-in is product and protocol specific. Furthermore, it operates in a way similar to RBAC/ABAC systems.

We see, therefore, that our proposed approach, while it seems similar to many existing and proposed solutions, is significantly different, designed specifically for the IoT, and very flexible, allowing its effortless integration with diverse existing business systems and applications, or its incorporation into new IoT system or application designs.

7   Conclusions

In this paper we presented a security solution for an interoperable IoT architecture. The proposed solution achieves endpoint authentication, user authorization, and key establishment between two endpoints. The proposed solution relies on a third party referred to as the Access Control Provider (ACP). The ACP, which can be implemented alongside the user management system of a company, guarantees that no user specific information is stored in Things. Moreover, the ACP allows users to securely communicate with Things without any pre-established secret information. By storing access control policies in ACPs, our solution facilitates security management, since a modification to an access control policy does not have to be propagated to the involved Things. Moreover, by hiding business logic from Things, Business-to-Business services are facilitated.

The proposed solution can be seamlessly integrated with (D)TLS. In particular, we leveraged specific fields of the (D)TLS handshake protocol (without breaking their semantics) to transfer our protocol specific parameters. Then we used the (D)TLS key derivation function to securely create an encryption key that can be used for protecting the integrity and the confidentiality of all subsequent messages. This integration is important for many reasons: it facilitates application development, since existing applications based on (D)TLS can be easily ported to our system, it enhances the security of our approach, and it provides a mechanism for (D)TLS to create pre-shared keys.

As a proof of concept, we incorporated our solution to the INTER-IoT interoperable gateway and we extended its API. Our extensions allow INTER-IoT gateway-based systems to include existing user management systems with very little effort. Given the security requirements of the scenarios considered by the INTER-IoT team, this is an important development since involved stakeholders do not have to allow third parties to access their (critical) security systems.

Acknowledgment. This work was funded through INTER-IoT Collaboration Agreement #52 (ACHILLES), which is administered through AUEB-RC. INTER-IoT has received funding from the EC through programme H2020. The paper presents the views of the authors and not necessarily those of the EC or the INTER-IoT consortium.

References

1. Anti-Rivalry definition. https://wiki.p2pfoundation.net/Anti-Rivalry. Accessed 8 July 2018
2. Authentication plugin for Mosquitto with multiple back-ends. https://github.com/jpmens/mosquitto-auth-plug. Accessed 8 July 2018
3. Eclipse Keti. https://projects.eclipse.org/proposals/eclipse-keti. Accessed 8 July 2018
4. INTER-IoT project home page. http://www.inter-iot-project.eu. Accessed 8 July 2018
5. Blazquez, A., Tsiatsis, V., Vandikas, K.: Performance evaluation of openID connect for an IoT information marketplace. In: 2015 IEEE 81st Vehicular Technology Conference (VTC Spring), pp. 1–6 (2015)
6. Cirani, S., Picone, M., Gonizzi, P., Veltri, L., Ferrari, G.: IoT-OAS: an OAuth-based authorization service architecture for secure services in IoT scenarios. IEEE Sens. J. **15**(2), 1224–1234 (2015)
7. Eronen, P., Tschofenig, H.: Pre-shared key ciphersuites for transport layer security (TLS). RFC 4729, IETF (2005)
8. Ferraiolo, D.F., Sandhu, R., Gavrila, S., Kuhn, D.R., Chandramouli, R.: Proposed NIST standard for role-based access control. ACM Trans. Inf. Syst. Secur. **4**(3), 224–274 (2001)
9. Fotiou, N., Kotsonis, T., Marias, G.F., Polyzos, G.C.: Access control for the Internet of Things. In: 2016 ESORICS International Workshop on Secure Internet of Things (SIoT), pp. 29–38 (2016)

10. Gusmeroli, S., Piccione, S., Rotondi, D.: A capability-based security approach to manage access control in the Internet of Things. Math. Comput. Model. **58**(5), 1189–1205 (2013). The Measurement of Undesirable Outputs: Models Development and Empirical Analyses and Advances in mobile, ubiquitous and cognitive computing
11. Hardt, D. (ed.): The OAuth 2.0 Authorization Framework. RFC 6749, IETF (2012)
12. Recordon, D., Reed, D.: OpenID 2.0: a platform for user-centric identity management. In: Proceedings of the Second ACM Workshop on Digital Identity Management, DIM 2006, New York, NY, USA, pp. 11–16 (2006)
13. Rescorla, E., Modadugu, N.: Datagram transport layer security version 1.2. RFC 6347, IETF (2012)
14. Seitz, L., Selander, G., Gehrmann, C.: Authorization framework for the Internet-of-Things. In: 2013 IEEE 14th International Symposium and Workshops on a Mobile and Multimedia Networks (WoWMoM), World of Wireless, pp. 1–6. IEEE Computer Society, Los Alamitos (2013)
15. Shelby, Z., Hartke, K., Bormann, C.: The Constrained Application Protocol (CoAP). RFC 7252, IETF (2014)

Bringing Access Control Tree to Big Data

Francesco Di Cerbo[1(✉)] and Marco Rosa[1,2]

[1] SAP Security Research, Sophia Antipolis, France
francesco.di.cerbo@sap.com
[2] Università degli Studi di Bergamo, Bergamo, Italy
marco.rosa@unibg.it

Abstract. Big data architectures bring advantages in terms of analytics performances and data storage. However the scarce availability of highly expressive declarative mechanisms for access control limits certain business and technical possibilities. This paper reports on the extension and adaptation of Access Control Tree to support effective decision making processes especially in evaluating multiple data policies for large data sets. An initial evaluation is also presented to evaluate the applicability of the extensions to big data use cases.

Keywords: Access control · Big data · Access control tree

1 Introduction

Data management, and especially control, is a crucial aspect for data owners when they adopt cloud solutions, especially from public infrastructures. IoT, social media, user's profiling tools are just few examples of information sources that produce significant amount of data to be processed and analyzed, often on big data architectures on cloud (public) infrastructures. The nature of these data (sometimes personal information, sometimes sensitive for other profiles) normally compels data owners to adopt strict security measures to protect against information leaks and abuses. Access control is a key measure in this respect.

However, modern access control mechanisms for big data have often to mediate against conflicting requirements, trading off granularity and performance. Expressiveness in access control configuration comes at the expenses of performance and therefore, declarative approaches do not seem to be suitable. Let us consider the case of the Hadoop family and Apache Ranger[1]. It offers a central configuration with a number of plug-ins for the different components of the Hadoop software family. However the characteristics of the enforcement and the configuration granularity are very different from component to component, but they hardly seem to meet the expressiveness of XACML [6] policies even though they support models like RBAC.

---

[1] https://ranger.apache.org/.

© Springer Nature Switzerland AG 2018
A. Saracino and P. Mori (Eds.): ETAA 2018, LNCS 11263, pp. 17–29, 2018.
https://doi.org/10.1007/978-3-030-04372-8_2

In this space, our proposal goes in the direction of extending a high-speed caching access control tree (the Access Control Tree) that accelerates the decision making process (compared with XACML traditional approaches) without impacting on the consistency of the rules. In particular, we focus on the support of a relevant use case for big data applications: the evaluation of access control decisions on a set of resources, each with their own data-specific policy.

Outline. The remainder of this paper is organized as follows. Section 2 introduces the problem we are aiming to address with this work. Section 3 introduces the Access Control Tree concept. Section 4 instead illustrates our contribution to extend the ACT concept, by introducing two new algorithms, respectively in Sects. 4.1 and 4.2, together with an initial performance evaluation and an example. Lastly, Sect. 5 discusses some related works while Sect. 6 presents our conclusions.

2   The Problem

Big data architectures store significant amount of data and offer efficient methods to analyze them. Architectures like Lambda [4] allow for computing analytics in streaming or in batch mode, according to whether one demands a real-time overview or a more sound, detailed analysis on data produced by the information sources of interest. Data clustering, aggregation, classification operations are normally highly used in such contexts.

However, such analysis normally requires full control on input data. It is well possible that pieces of information collected from different information sources may have different exploitation possibilities. Certain information may be confidential, or simply not accessible by specific users or user roles. Regulating access on different data with different access requirements, especially in Lambda architectures requires extremely efficient access control solutions, able to evaluate requests to access multiple (in the range of thousands up to millions) resources at the same time. The peak of this complexity is reached when each of the requested resources has its own policy, as it may be the case for resources involving Personally Identifiable Information (PII).

We claim that big data architectures need advanced access control systems, capable of:

R1. Consider requests for high number of resources (100k+) at the same time.
R2. Evaluate requests with response time one order of magnitude smaller than the requested analytics.

This paper presents our current activities working for the implementation of these requirements.

3   Access Control Tree

The Access Control Tree (ACT) is a methodology to cache access control directives, able to make extremely fast runtime decisions; its implementations have demonstrated response times of few milliseconds for thousands of requests [1, 7]. To achieve this result, ACT takes advantage of policies and rules aggregation in order to build a tree data structure that can be explored in order to evaluate an access control request.

In particular, ACT consists of 2 algorithms:

a. *Insertion*, that allows for the creation/update of an ACT from an XACML policy.
b. *Request*, that permits to evaluate a request as a tree exploration of the ACT.

The *Insertion* algorithm permits to transform an XACML policy in the form of a Permission (or Deny) tree. The components of a policy's *Rule* (*Target*'s {*Subject, Action, Resource*} and *Condition*) become nodes of a tree structure and the *Insertion* algorithm describes how to compose the tree. If the tree is structured with subjects as first-level elements, the branches stemming from each of the subjects represent the permitted actions and for what resources. It derives that the *Request* algorithm describes how to process a request, as a simple exploration of the ACT structure.

In cases where one or more XACML policies are used to control a system, the application of ACT requires:

a. The execution of the *Insertion* algorithm as preliminary operation.
b. At runtime, the execution of the *Request* algorithm to evaluate access requests.

4   Contribution

The work described in this article deals with the fulfillment of the two requirements **R1** and **R2** as expressed in Sect. 2. In order to approach the problem, let us consider the following working hypotheses:

H1. ACT nodes represent disjoint elements.
H2. Request elements can always be associated with one and only one of the ACT nodes.
H3. Each requested resource has its own policy, therefore its own ACT.

The **H1** expresses the condition that each ACT node can be associated with one and only one element of a policy expressed in XACML. Situations like usage of RBAC rules (e.g. "Doctors can read medical records") mixed with individual rules ("Dr. Jones can read medical records") are not yet supported, while the adoption of either of the models is compatible with ACT. Similarly to policies, also request elements can unequivocally be associated with one ACT element **H2**. The third hypothesis **H3** is specific to the big data use case we are considering: each of the individual resources referenced by an access control request is regulated by its own policy.

In order to support the evaluation of requests addressing multiple resources, each with their own access policy, our contribution consists of:

– an algorithm to merge multiple ACTs into a single one (the *Merge* algorithm).
– an extended Request algorithm, called *Request Multiple Resources* to evaluate requests dealing with multiple resources, as in big data architectures.

An ACT-based mechanism for big data will apply the new algorithms as follows:

1. pre-compute all policies of all resources
2. merge the resulting ACTs with the *Merge* algorithm, either in *pre-computation* or at *runtime* when a request targeting multiple resources occurs.
3. evaluate such request using the extended *Request Multiple Resources* algorithm.

The following sections will detail the new algorithms.

4.1   The Merge Algorithm

The *Merge* algorithm considers a number of ACTs as described in Sect. 3, composed of *Subjects, Actions, Resources* and *Conditions*. ACTs are created using the *Insertion* mechanism as described in [7], while the *Merge* algorithm is listed in Algorithm 1. It essentially considers one empty ACT that gets new branches as the algorithm iterates over each other ACT, when the branches (at the different level: *Subject, Action, Resource* or *Condition*) are not part of the initial ACT. Interestingly, this algorithm works identically also for non-specific rules (transformed in ACT as nodes labeled as *Any*).

Figure 1 shows an example of the *Merge* algorithm on two ACTs.

Evaluation. We evaluated the performance of the merge algorithm. We considered in particular the two requirements **R1** and **R2**, therefore we applied the *Merge* algorithm on sets of 100, 1000, 10000 and 100000 randomly generated policies with a number of subjects in [1–5], actions in [1–5], resources in [2–1000000] in order to generate complex merging conditions. Figure 2 shows a logarithmic trend in the number of input ACTs. It is worth noting that the algorithm and ACT implementations were not optimized and were only using basic Java 8 data structures and constructs. The evaluation was conducted on an Intel Core i7 4790 CPU (4 Haswell Cores, 3.75 GHz), 16 GB of System Memory, a 240 GB PCI-EX SSD.

4.2   The Request Multiple Resources Algorithm

Once the merged ACT is created, it is ready to evaluate access requests. Such requests may come in different ways:

1. XACML requests targeting a single resource are evaluated as described in [1, 7], with a simple tree exploration.
2. as prescribed by [5], it is possible to create multiple decision requests. In such cases, the *Request Multiple Resources* algorithm is used and the decision may be *combined*, i.e., only one answer will be returned if and only if the decisions for all requests are identical, or the response may be composed of a set of individual decisions for each of the requests.

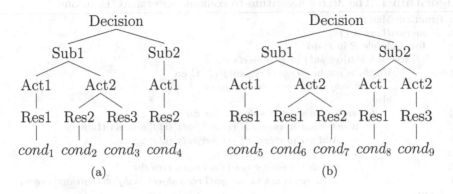

(a)   (b)

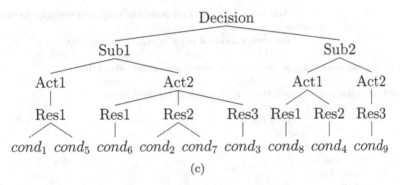

(c)

Fig. 1. Result of the merge (Fig. 1c) of two decision trees (Fig. 1a and b)

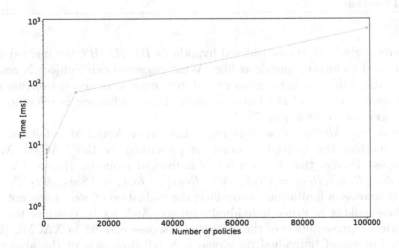

Fig. 2. The time interval required for computing the Merge algorithm for merging 100, 1000, 10000 and 100000 ACTs

---

Algorithm 1. The *Merge* algorithm to combine several ACTs in one.

```
1: function MERGE(P)
2:      mergedTree = {}
3:      for each rule R in P do
4:          for each subject subj in R.subjects do
5:              if subj is not in mergedTree.subjects then
6:                  Add subj in mergedTree.subjects
7:              else
8:                  for each action act in subj.actions do
9:                      if act is not in mergedTree.subjects[subj].actions then
10:                         Add act in mergedTree.subjects[subj].actions
11:                     else
12:                         for each resource res in act.resources do
13:                             if res is not in mergedTree.subjects[subj].actions[act].resources
    then
14:                                 Add res in mergedTree.subjects[subj].actions[act].resources
15:                             else
16:                                 for each condition cond in res.conditions do
17:                                     if         cond        is        not        in
    mergedTree.subjects[subj].actions[act].resources[res].conditions then
18:                                         Add           cond           in
    mergedTree.subjects[subj].actions[act].resources[res].conditions
19:                                     end if
20:                                 end for
21:                             end if
22:                         end for
23:                     end if
24:                 end for
25:             end if
26:         end for
27:     end for
28:     Return mergedTree
29: end function
```

Interestingly, with the considered hypothesis *H1, H2, H3*, the merged ACT may be used to answer questions like "What resources can Subject X read?", i.e., the ACT will be able to enumerate all resources in an access response even if they were not part of the initial request. This mechanism is referenced by practitioners as "reverse query"[2].

The *Request Multiple Resources* algorithm can be described as follows.
Let us consider the multiple request as prescribed by the XACML Multiple Request Profile, that is, as a set of individual requests: $Req = \{Req_1 = \{Sub_1, Act_1, Res_1\}, Req_2 = \{Sub_1, Act_1, Res_2\} \ldots Req_n = \{Sub_1, Act_1, Res_n\}\}$. There is however a limitation to consider: the evaluation of Req_i must not have conditions looking at other individual requests. And, let us consider that the appropriate representation of the requested response context in XACML (be it combined or set of individual decisions) is handled outside of the algorithm.

---

[2] see for example: https://www.axiomatics.com/blog/blimey-what-s-axiomatics-reverse-query/.

Algorithm 2. Request evaluation (*individual decisions*)

```
1: function EVALUATE(Req)
2:     Req = {Sub_1, Act_1, [Res_1, Res_2, Res_3 ... Res_N]}
3:     DT = DecisionTree
4:     if Sub_1 not exists in DT.subjects then
5:         Return Deny
6:     else
7:         if Act_1 not exists in DT.subjects[Sub_1].actions then
8:             Return Deny
9:         else
10:            for r_i ← Res_1, Res_n do                    ▷ parallel execution
11:                if the conditions for the request {Sub_1, Act_1, r_i} are satisfied then
12:                    Return Permit for {Sub_1, Act_1, r_1}
13:                else
14:                    Return Deny for {Sub_1, Act_1, r_1}
15:                end if
16:            end for
17:        end if
18:    end if
19: end function
```

Algorithm 3. Request evaluation (*combined decision*)

```
1: function EVALUATE(Req)
2:     Req = {Sub_1, Act_1, [Res_1, Res_2, Res_3 ... Res_N]}
3:     DT = DecisionTree
4:     if Sub_1 not exists in DT.subjects then
5:         Return Deny
6:     else
7:         if Act_1 not exists in DT.subjects[Sub_1].actions then
8:             Return Deny
9:         else
10:            for r_i ← Res_1, Res_n do
11:                if the conditions for the request {Sub_1, Act_1, r_i} are not satisfied
    then
12:                    Return Deny for {Sub_1, Act_1, [Res_1, Res_2, Res_3 ... Res_N]}
13:                end if
14:            end for
15:            Return Permit for {Sub_1, Act_1, [Res_1, Res_2, Res_3 ... Res_N]}
16:        end if
17:    end if
18: end function
```

Let us define an equivalent notation for *Req*, an aggregation operation on the request context. $Req = Sub_1, Act_1, [Res_1, Res_2, \ldots, Res_n]$. The algorithm has two different versions, for individual or combined decision requests.

- The individual decision algorithm is depicted in Algorithm 2. It can be easily parallelized, considering as execution tokens each of the individual requests

$r_i = \{Sub_i, Act_j, [Res_1, \ldots, Res_n]\}$. It returns to the component in charge of creating the XACML response a result for each of the r_i execution flows, as they can be evaluated independently.

- The combined decision request is represented in Algorithm 3. As in the previous case, each r_i can be evaluated in parallel in order to save execution time, but the single responses need to be collected and combined together in order to ensure that all of them result in a *Permit*. Even one single *Deny* causes a negative final response to the user.

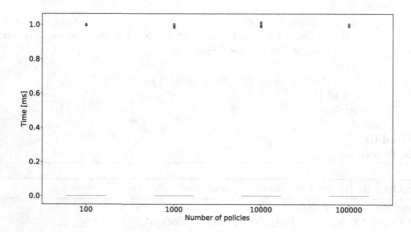

Fig. 3. The time interval required for processing requests against a merged ACT generated by 100, 1000, 10000 and 100000 policies

Example. Figure 4 shows an example of the evaluation flow of a request onto a merged ACT. We define a sample ACT with two subjects $Subj_1$ and $Subj_2$, two actions Act_1 and Act_2, two resources Res_1 and Res_2, and several conditions as shown in Fig. 4a. At the beginning we consider our token to be at the root of the ACT (the decision level). We consider a request of the form $\{Subj_1, Act_1, Res_1\}$. This produces an exploration in the tree, moving the token respectively to Sub_1 (Fig. 4b), Act_1 (Fig. 4c), and Res_1 (Fig. 4d). Finally, depending on the requested decision (combined or individual), the token navigates the conditions in series (Fig. 4e and f) or in parallel (Fig. 4g).

Evaluation. The algorithm was evaluated with respect to its performance, in the same setting as described in Sect. 4.1. The results of the evaluation are shown in Fig. 3. In line with previous results [1,7], a request evaluation mapped as tree exploration (when applicable policies do not contain conditions to evaluate) results in a practically immediate operation. The evaluation was conducted using 4 different ACTs generated using 100, 1000, 10000 and 100000 XACML policies, against 1000 requests randomly generated. The mean execution time stays close to 0.01 ms, besides a number of outliers between 4 and 8 (for the ACT with 1000 policies).

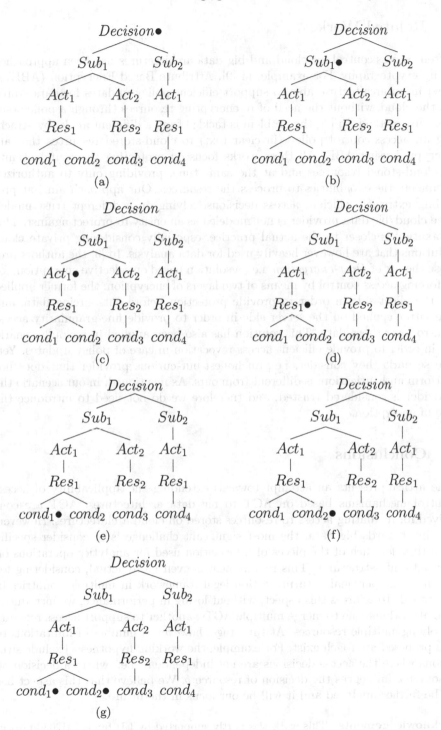

Fig. 4. Example of the flow of a request evaluation

5   Related Work

Often, access control for cloud and big data architectures has been approached using cryptography. For example, in [9], Attribute Based Encryption (ABE) is used in an architecture able to support efficient policy updates for data stored on the cloud, without the need of re-encrypting resources through a policy outsourcing method. In [8], the problem is tackled from a different angle, by attaching an access control policy (in clear text) to cloud-stored resources that are encrypted using ABE. All these works focus on protecting the confidentiality of cloud-stored resources and at the same time, providing only to authorized recipients the capabilities to process the resources. Our approach aims at providing extremely efficient access decisions, relying on a different trust model. The cloud/big data provider is not modeled as an entity to protect against. This relaxation is closer to the actual practice, especially considering private cloud solutions that are however heavily used for data analysis. In [3] the authors propose the use of *Over-encryption*, i.e., a solution based on selective encryption, for enforcing access control by means of two layers of encryption: the former applied on the client side in order to provide protection before outsourcing data, and the latter applied on the server side in order to provide fine-granularity access control over those data. This solution has also been applied in a cloud scenario [2] in order to provide efficient access revocation in case of policy updates. Yet, the scenario they consider, i.e., an honest-but-curious provider that does not perform authentication, is different from ours. As mentioned, in our scenario the provider is considered trusted, and therefore we do not need to introduce the use of encryption.

6   Conclusions

The article presents an attempt towards extending the applicability of access control mechanisms based on ACT to big data architectures. ACT are conceived for regulating access to resources stored on cloud architectures. However, moving towards big data, the most significant challenge is to consider specific directives for each of the pieces of information used for analytics operations on big data infrastructures. This requirement is even more actual, considering for example the personal data protection legal framework in multiple countries in the world. To address this aspect, without losing in performance, we introduced two algorithms, one to merge multiple ACTs, another to support access requests involving multiple resources. At this stage, however, a number of limitations to the proposed approach exist. For example, the working hypothesis exclude situations where the access decisions are not independent, i.e., where a decision on resource a influences the decision of resource b. We believe that this aspect has to be further analyzed and it will be our focus in the future.

Acknowledgements. This work was partly supported by EU-funded H2020 project C3ISP [grant no. 700294].

Appendix

```
<Policy xmlns="urn:oasis:names:tc:xacml:3.0:core:schema:wd-17" PolicyId="policyR57"
    ↪ RuleCombiningAlgId="urn:oasis:names:tc:xacml:1.0:rule-combining-algorithm:permit-
    ↪ overrides" Version="3.0">
  <Target/>
  <Rule Effect="Permit" RuleId="Permit-R57">
    <Description>R57</Description>
    <Target>
      <AnyOf>
        <AllOf>
          <Match MatchId="urn:oasis:names:tc:xacml:1.0:function:string-equal">
            <AttributeValue DataType="http://www.w3.org/2001/XMLSchema#string">A3</
                ↪ AttributeValue><AttributeDesignator AttributeId="
                ↪ urn:oasis:names:tc:xacml:1.0:action:action-id" Category="
                ↪ urn:oasis:names:tc:xacml:3.0:attribute-category:action" DataType="
                ↪ http://www.w3.org/2001/XMLSchema#string" MustBePresent="false"/></
                ↪ Match>
          <Match MatchId="urn:oasis:names:tc:xacml:1.0:function:string-equal">
            <AttributeValue DataType="http://www.w3.org/2001/XMLSchema#string">S1</
                ↪ AttributeValue><AttributeDesignator AttributeId="
                ↪ urn:oasis:names:tc:xacml:1.0:subject:subject-id" Category="
                ↪ urn:oasis:names:tc:xacml:1.0:subject-category:access-subject"
                ↪ DataType="http://www.w3.org/2001/XMLSchema#string" MustBePresent="
                ↪ false"/></Match>
          <Match MatchId="urn:oasis:names:tc:xacml:1.0:function:string-equal">
            <AttributeValue DataType="http://www.w3.org/2001/XMLSchema#string">R57</
                ↪ AttributeValue><AttributeDesignator AttributeId="
                ↪ urn:oasis:names:tc:xacml:1.0:resource:resource-id" Category="
                ↪ urn:oasis:names:tc:xacml:3.0:attribute-category:resource" DataType="
                ↪ http://www.w3.org/2001/XMLSchema#string" MustBePresent="false"/></
                ↪ Match>
        </AllOf>
      </AnyOf>
    </Target>
  </Rule>
  <Rule Effect="Permit" RuleId="Permit-R57-1">
    <Description>R57-1</Description>
    <Target>
      <AnyOf>
        <AllOf>
          <Match MatchId="urn:oasis:names:tc:xacml:1.0:function:string-equal">
            <AttributeValue DataType="http://www.w3.org/2001/XMLSchema#string">A3</
                ↪ AttributeValue><AttributeDesignator AttributeId="
                ↪ urn:oasis:names:tc:xacml:1.0:action:action-id" Category="
                ↪ urn:oasis:names:tc:xacml:3.0:attribute-category:action" DataType="
                ↪ http://www.w3.org/2001/XMLSchema#string" MustBePresent="false"/></
                ↪ Match>
          <Match MatchId="urn:oasis:names:tc:xacml:1.0:function:string-equal">
            <AttributeValue DataType="http://www.w3.org/2001/XMLSchema#string">S2</
                ↪ AttributeValue><AttributeDesignator AttributeId="
                ↪ urn:oasis:names:tc:xacml:1.0:subject:subject-id" Category="
                ↪ urn:oasis:names:tc:xacml:1.0:subject-category:access-subject"
                ↪ DataType="http://www.w3.org/2001/XMLSchema#string" MustBePresent="
                ↪ false"/></Match>
          <Match MatchId="urn:oasis:names:tc:xacml:1.0:function:string-equal">
            <AttributeValue DataType="http://www.w3.org/2001/XMLSchema#string">R57</
                ↪ AttributeValue><AttributeDesignator AttributeId="
                ↪ urn:oasis:names:tc:xacml:1.0:resource:resource-id" Category="
                ↪ urn:oasis:names:tc:xacml:3.0:attribute-category:resource" DataType="
                ↪ http://www.w3.org/2001/XMLSchema#string" MustBePresent="false"/></
                ↪ Match>
        </AllOf>
      </AnyOf>
    </Target>
  </Rule>
  <Rule Effect="Permit" RuleId="Permit-R57-2">
```

```
        <Description>R57-2</Description>
        <Target>
          <AnyOf>
            <AllOf>
              <Match MatchId="urn:oasis:names:tc:xacml:1.0:function:string-equal">
                <AttributeValue DataType="http://www.w3.org/2001/XMLSchema#string">A2</
                  ↪ AttributeValue><AttributeDesignator AttributeId="
                  ↪ urn:oasis:names:tc:xacml:1.0:action:action-id" Category="
                  ↪ urn:oasis:names:tc:xacml:3.0:attribute-category:action" DataType="
                  ↪ http://www.w3.org/2001/XMLSchema#string" MustBePresent="false"/></
                  ↪ Match>
              <Match MatchId="urn:oasis:names:tc:xacml:1.0:function:string-equal">
                <AttributeValue DataType="http://www.w3.org/2001/XMLSchema#string">S1</
                  ↪ AttributeValue><AttributeDesignator AttributeId="
                  ↪ urn:oasis:names:tc:xacml:1.0:subject:subject-id" Category="
                  ↪ urn:oasis:names:tc:xacml:1.0:subject-category:access-subject"
                  ↪ DataType="http://www.w3.org/2001/XMLSchema#string" MustBePresent="
                  ↪ false"/></Match>
              <Match MatchId="urn:oasis:names:tc:xacml:1.0:function:string-equal">
                <AttributeValue DataType="http://www.w3.org/2001/XMLSchema#string">R57</
                  ↪ AttributeValue><AttributeDesignator AttributeId="
                  ↪ urn:oasis:names:tc:xacml:1.0:resource:resource-id" Category="
                  ↪ urn:oasis:names:tc:xacml:3.0:attribute-category:resource" DataType="
                  ↪ http://www.w3.org/2001/XMLSchema#string" MustBePresent="false"/></
                  ↪ Match>
            </AllOf>
          </AnyOf>
        </Target>
      </Rule>
      <Rule Effect="Permit" RuleId="Permit-R57-3">
        <Description>R57-3</Description>
        <Target>
          <AnyOf>
            <AllOf>
              <Match MatchId="urn:oasis:names:tc:xacml:1.0:function:string-equal">
                <AttributeValue DataType="http://www.w3.org/2001/XMLSchema#string">A2</
                  ↪ AttributeValue><AttributeDesignator AttributeId="
                  ↪ urn:oasis:names:tc:xacml:1.0:action:action-id" Category="
                  ↪ urn:oasis:names:tc:xacml:3.0:attribute-category:action" DataType="
                  ↪ http://www.w3.org/2001/XMLSchema#string" MustBePresent="false"/></
                  ↪ Match>
              <Match MatchId="urn:oasis:names:tc:xacml:1.0:function:string-equal">
                <AttributeValue DataType="http://www.w3.org/2001/XMLSchema#string">S2</
                  ↪ AttributeValue><AttributeDesignator AttributeId="
                  ↪ urn:oasis:names:tc:xacml:1.0:subject:subject-id" Category="
                  ↪ urn:oasis:names:tc:xacml:1.0:subject-category:access-subject"
                  ↪ DataType="http://www.w3.org/2001/XMLSchema#string" MustBePresent="
                  ↪ false"/></Match>
              <Match MatchId="urn:oasis:names:tc:xacml:1.0:function:string-equal">
                <AttributeValue DataType="http://www.w3.org/2001/XMLSchema#string">R57</
                  ↪ AttributeValue><AttributeDesignator AttributeId="
                  ↪ urn:oasis:names:tc:xacml:1.0:resource:resource-id" Category="
                  ↪ urn:oasis:names:tc:xacml:3.0:attribute-category:resource" DataType="
                  ↪ http://www.w3.org/2001/XMLSchema#string" MustBePresent="false"/></
                  ↪ Match>
            </AllOf>
          </AnyOf>
        </Target>
      </Rule>
      <Rule Effect="Deny" RuleId="Deny-R57"/>
    </Policy>
```

References

1. Ayeb, N., Di Cerbo, F., Trabelsi, S.: Enhancing access control trees for cloud computing. In: Casteleyn, S., Dolog, P., Pautasso, C. (eds.) ICWE 2016. LNCS, vol. 9881, pp. 29–38. Springer, Cham (2016). https://doi.org/10.1007/978-3-319-46963-8_3
2. Bacis, E., De Capitani di Vimercati, S., Foresti, S., Paraboschi, S., Rosa, M., Samarati, P.: Access control management for secure cloud storage. In: Deng, R., Weng, J., Ren, K., Yegneswaran, V. (eds.) SecureComm 2016. LNICSSITE, vol. 198, pp. 353–372. Springer, Cham (2017). https://doi.org/10.1007/978-3-319-59608-2_21
3. De Capitani di Vimercati, S., Foresti, S., Jajodia, S., Paraboschi, S., Samarati, P.: Over-encryption: management of access control evolution on outsourced data. In: Proceedings of the 33rd International Conference on Very Large Data Bases (VLDB 2007), Vienna, Austria, pp. 123–134, September 2007
4. Marz, N., Warren, J.: Big Data: Principles and Best Practices of Scalable Real-Time Data Systems. Manning Publications Co., New York (2015)
5. OASIS Committee Draft: XACML v3.0 multiple decision profile (2010). https://docs.oasis-open.org/xacml/3.0/xacml-3.0-multiple-v1-spec-cd-03-en.html. Accessed 10 July 2018
6. OASIS Standard: Extensible Access Control Markup Language (XACML) Version 3.0 (2013–2017). https://docs.oasis-open.org/xacml/3.0/errata01/os/xacml-3.0-core-spec-errata01-os-complete.html. Accessed 10 July 2018
7. Trabelsi, S., Ecuyer, A., Cervera y Alvarez, P., Di Cerbo, F.: Optimizing access control performance for the cloud. In: Proceedings of the 4th International Conference on Cloud Computing and Services Science (CLOSER 2014), Barcelona, Spain, pp. 551–558, April 2014
8. Yang, K., Han, Q., Li, H., Zheng, K., Su, Z., Shen, X.: An efficient and fine-grained big data access control scheme with privacy-preserving policy. IEEE Internet of Things J. 4(2), 563–571 (2017)
9. Yang, K., Jia, X., Ren, K.: Secure and verifiable policy update outsourcing for big data access control in the cloud. IEEE Trans. Parallel Distrib. Syst. 26(12), 3461–3470 (2015)

SNAPAUTH: A Gesture-Based Unobtrusive Smartwatch User Authentication Scheme

Attaullah Buriro[1,2]([⊠])([iD]), Bruno Crispo[1,3], Mojtaba Eskandri[4],
Sandeep Gupta[1], Athar Mahboob[2], and Rutger Van Acker[5]

[1] Department of Information Engineering and Computer Science (DISI),
University of Trento, Trento, Italy
{attaullah.buriro,bruno.crispo,sandeep.gupta}@unitn.it
[2] Department of Information Security, Khwaja Fareed University of Engineering and
Information Technology, Rahim Yar Khan, Pakistan
[3] Department of Computer Science, DistriNET, KU Lueven, Leuven, Belgium
[4] Create-NET, Foundazione Bruno Kessler (FBK), Trento, Italy
[5] Swift via Exellys, Hamont-Achel Hamont, Flanders, Belgium

Abstract. In this paper, we present a novel motion-based behavioral biometric-based user authentication solution - SNAPAUTH, for Android-based smartwatch. SNAPAUTH requires the user to perform finger-snapping (Snapping (or clicking) one's fingers is the act of creating a snapping or clicking sound with one's fingers. Primarily this is done by building tension between the thumb and another (middle, index, or ring) finger and then moving the other finger forcefully downward so it hits the palm of the same hand at a high speed [4].) action, while wearing the smartwatch to perform the authentication. SNAPAUTH profiles the arm-movements by collecting data from smartwatch's built-in accelerometer and gyroscope sensors, while the user performs this action. We implemented and evaluated SNAPAUTH on Motorola Moto 3G smartwatch. SNAPAUTH could be widely accepted by users as it utilizes the users' familiarity with the very common finger-snapping action and users do not need to remember any secret.

Keywords: Security · Authentication and access control
Behavioral biometrics · Smartwatch

1 Introduction

The use of smartwatches is steadily and constantly increasing in recent years. Since, they are typically a personal device that users hold all the time, they are an obvious candidate device to support authentication of its owner.

Authentication is the process of restricting the device access to the legitimate users, only.

Classical authentication schemes, such as PIN/password establish the identity with what the user remembers. These solutions are neither considered secure [1] nor usable [2,3], because they require users to remember their secret

© Springer Nature Switzerland AG 2018
A. Saracino and P. Mori (Eds.): ETAA 2018, LNCS 11263, pp. 30–37, 2018.
https://doi.org/10.1007/978-3-030-04372-8_3

and enter it every time they need to use the device. Additionally, entering text or sketching a graphical password on smartwatches could be extremely difficult because of the small size of the touchscreen.

Biometric-based authentication establish the identity through biological modalities, such as face, fingerprint, retina, etc. These solutions have already been implemented on recent smartphones, e.g., Apple Face ID [5] and fingerprint sensors in iPhones [6], however, these schemes, being non-transparent, have still the main disadvantage of annoying the user [7]. Further, the data of some of these modalities can be stolen as easily as passwords [10].

Behavioral biometric, e.g., swiping, touch-dynamics, etc., seems a better option for the development of user authentication schemes for the new generation of personal devices, because they are dependent on the person-specific user actions and habits, which makes them more attractive towards implicit/unobtrusive user authentication [11].

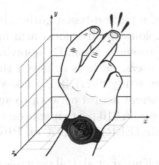

Fig. 1. Finger-snapping in 3d space

In this work, we present a motion-based finger-snapping gesture-based user authentication scheme - SnapAuth, for smartwatch unlocking. The scheme collects the arm movements fingerprints through the accelerometer and gyroscope sensors in three dimensions, while the user performs the finger-snapping gesture (as depicted in Fig. 1), and performs user profiling. More specifically SnapAuth collects the arm-movement generated data, from accelerometer and gyroscope, for the short duration, during finger-snapping gesture, at a sample rate of 50 samples/s and performs the identity confirmation. SnapAuth, using simple, yet effective, state-of-the-art machine learning classifiers, decides if the smartwatch is worn by the legitimate user or by an impostor. Access to the smartwatch is granted in case the user is confirmed as the legitimate user otherwise its denied. SnapAuth neither requires any token or password from the user, thus, the scheme is completely unobtrusive, and usable for smartwatch unlocking. We validated SnapAuth on a real device (Motorola Moto 3G) and obtained promising results.

The main contributions of this paper are:

- The proposal of SNAPAUTH - an arm-motion-based user authentication scheme for Android smartwatch. The scheme authenticates the users based on the differences in the arm-movements generated while user performs finger-snapping action.
- Proof-of-the-concept prototype implementation of the scheme on a smartwatch.

2   Related Work

Behavioral biometric-based user authentication using smartwatches has been already explored by few papers. Draw-a-pin [12] leverages the user behaviour while drawing a PIN and the correctness of the PIN, to authenticate the user. Authors achieved 20.36% average error rate on their collected dataset of 30 participants, in two activities, i.e., sitting, walking, in lab settings using Samsung Gear Live smartwatch.

Lewis et al. [13] proposed a motion-based authentication solution for smartwatch users. The system exploits the free-form arm movement as a behavioral biometric modality for user authentication. By applying DTW as a classifier on their collected dataset of 5 users, authors achieved the accuracy up to 84.6%. Similarly, the other relevant study "VeriNET", takes motion signals as password, and uses the deep recurrent neural network to authenticate the users [15]. Authors evaluated their scheme on 310 participants on $\approx$60k passcode entries and achieved an Equal Error Rate (EER) of 7.17% on PINs and 6.09% on Android lock patterns.

We consider the study by Kumar et al. [14] very relevant to our work. Authors proposed four variants of continuous user authentication design based on users arm movements while walking. The design incorporated smartwatchs accelerometer and gyroscope sensor data, individually as first and second variants, and then, applied feature and score-level fusion as the third and fourth variant. The system was tested under 3 different environments, i.e., intra-session (40 users dataset), inter-session (40 users dataset), and inter-phase (12 users dataset) using 4 classifiers, namely, k nearest neighbors (k-NN) with Euclidean distance, Logistic Regression, Multilayer Perceptrons, and Random Forest resulting in a total of sixteen authentication mechanisms. They achieved the mean dynamic False Accept Rate (DFAR) of 0% and Dynamic False Reject Rate (DFRR) of 0% for all of the twelve authentication mechanisms in the intra-session environment. In the inter-session environment, k-NN performed best with a mean DFAR of 2.2% and DFRR of 4.2% for a feature level fusion-based design. Whereas, in the inter-phase environment, the DFAR and DFRR increased to 15.03% and 14.62% respectively for the same feature level fusion-based design with the k-NN classifier.

SNAPAUTH is different from existing state-of-the-art authentication solutions in the following ways: (i) it leverages a novel finger-snapping action that is easy to perform, and (ii) the data collection is fully unobtrusive making it suitable for designing frictionless user authentication solutions.

3   Methodology

In this section, we discuss the steps taken to design SnapAuth.

3.1   Considered Hardware

This work uses the Motorola Moto 360 smartwatch for implementation of the proposed authentication scheme. For both data collection and the validation phase, the considered sensors offered by the smartwatch are used for the generation of raw sensor data.

3.2   Smartwatch Sensors

Android categorizes built-in sensors in three types, i.e. motion, environmental and positional, in their API guide on sensors[1]. To capture gestures, applications in this work uses two built-in motion sensors available on the Moto 360 to measure the acceleration, and rotation during the performance of a gesture. Moto 360 delivers a 50 Hz sampling rate for both the accelerometer and gyroscope meaning that both sensors are able to ideally generate 50 samples per second with an error margin around ±3 samples per second.

3.3   Data Collection

We developed a customized Android application, namely *SnapCollector* to collect the finger-snapping gesture. *SnapCollector* can be installed on any Android-based smartwatch having Android version 4.4 or higher, installed. We collected accelerometer and gyroscope readings at highest sample rate (50 Hz) because this sample rate was found empirically suitable for authentication purposes, in recent studies [18]. Figure 2 shows the main screen of our developed application.

Fig. 2. Main screen and settings

We recruited 11 volunteers (8 males) to participate in our three-day long three-session experiment. The participants had a background in computer science. We asked them about the natural hand and in which wrist they usually wear their watch.

We collected data from an experiment spanned over three-sessions. We ensured that all the recruited participants had to participate in these sessions on three consecutive days. The motivation was to check the performance of the gesture in intra-session and inter-session analysis (Fig. 3).

---

[1] https://developer.android.com/guide/topics/sensors/sensors_overview.html.

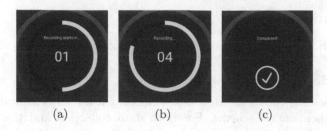

(a)   (b)   (c)

Fig. 3. (a) start of data recording & (b) data recording (c) recording complete.

3.4   Feature Extraction

The collected raw data from both accelerometer and gyroscope sensors is three dimensional, i.e., streams in X, Y, and Z dimensions. We also computed another dimension using the following equation and termed it as Magnitude.

$$S_m = \sqrt{s_x^2 + s_y^2 + s_z^2}$$

where S_m represents the magnitude of sensor S and s_x, s_y and s_z represent the values of the X, Y and Z stream respectively from sensor S. We extracted four statistical features, namely, mean(μ), standard deviation(σ), skewness(γ) and kurtosis(γ'), from every acquired raw stream and concatenate them to form a feature vector.

3.5   One-Class Classifier Selection

We chose three simple, yet effective state-of-the-art machine learning classifiers, namely, Bayes NET (BN); Multilayer Perceptron (MLP); and Random Forest (RF) to perform the classification. We chose these classifiers because they were found extremely accurate in the previous studies [16–18]. We used Weka workbench and used meta-class classifier - the *OneClassClassifier*[2], for our analysis.

4   Analysis

We collected 10 observations per activity per user (in total 50 observations in 5 activities). In first iteration, we picked the first two observations from each activity (just 10, in total) and trained the chosen classifiers on those observations. Remaining 40 observations were used as the testing set to perform the classification. In the second iteration, we picked 3 observations from each activity (15, in total) and trained the classifier on them, and the remaining 35 observations were used to test the classifier. We used max 15 observations for training, for two reasons: firstly because its common to get less number of training samples from

---

[2] http://weka.sourceforge.net/doc.packages/oneClassClassifier/weka/classifiers/
meta/OneClassClassifier.html.

users in real world, i.e., signature samples in banks, and secondly the users are reluctant to provide more training samples and might get annoyed if the system requires more training samples.

User authentication on smart devices is essentially a one-class classification problem where the data from one user - "the owner" is used to train the classifier and later that classifier is tested on the remaining samples of that one user - to obtain True Accept Rate (TAR) and False Reject Rate (FRR), and on the data of all the would-be adversaries (to obtain False Accept Rate (FAR) and True Reject Rate (TRR) [17]. We followed the above-mentioned scheme and trained all the chosen classifiers on the data of one user and tested in two settings (as mentioned above). The process is repeated for all the 11 users and the obtained average results are reported. Figure 4 drawn in the KnowledgeFlow module of Weka to perform both training and verification of One-class classifiers.

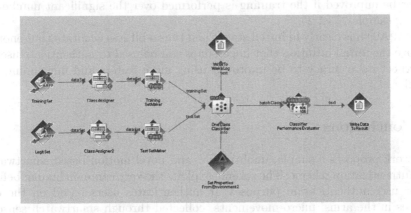

Fig. 4. Authentication scheme

5   Results

The accuracy of any biometric-based authentication system is normally reported in terms of TAR, FRR, FAR, or EER. We are reporting our obtained results in terms of TAR and FAR only as $TAR = 1 - FRR$ and $FAR = 1 - TRR$. Figure 5 depicts our obtained results (with default settings of all the classifiers) on full features.

MLP classifier performed comparatively better (see Fig. 5) as compared to its counterparts, i.e., BN and RF. We obtained 66.14% TAR at ≈27% FAR with default settings on just 10 training samples. TAR further improved with the increase in the number of training samples, i.e., training on 15 samples, provided 82.34% TAR, however, the FAR also increased (34.25%). The reason behind the increase of FAR is the less number of training samples and this could

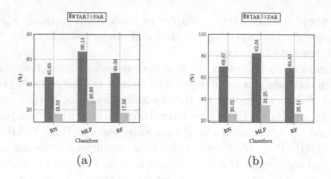

Fig. 5. Results of all the classifiers on 10 (a) & 15 (b) training samples.

further be improved if the training is performed over the significant number of training samples, i.e., 25.

SNAPAUTH is clearly in initial stages and thus a bit less accurate (but enough to prove the initial intuition that fingersnaps can be used to authenticate users). We expect its accuracy to be improved using more testers and fine tuning the classifier.

6 Conclusions

This work proposes a simple, unobtrusive, and novel motion-based smartwatch user authentication scheme. The scheme exploits the very common human behavior for user authentication purposes. It authenticates users based on the differences in the arms' micro-movements, collected through smartwatch sensors, while the user performs the finger-snapping action. SNAPAUTH is user-friendly and easy for the users because they do not require any secret to remember and/or to type. The scheme leverages the built-in hardware, so it does not require any additional dedicated hardware and hence avoids additional costs.

As future work, we are planning to repeat the experiments in the wild, possibly using a crowd-sourcing platform, thus increasing considerably the number of testers. We will also investigate and report the performance and usability of our scheme by performing usability related experiments. We will also perform accurate tests about the security of the scheme and how easy is for an attacker to spoof or mimic the behavior of legitimate users.

References

1. Lashkari, A.H., Farmand, S., Zakaria, D., Bin, O., Saleh, D.: Shoulder surfing attack in graphical password authentication. arXiv preprint: arXiv:0912.0951 (2009)
2. Davis, D., Monrose, F., Reiter, M.K.: On user choice in graphical password schemes. In: USENIX Security Symposium, vol. 13 (2004)

3. Gupta, S., Buriro, A., Crispo, B.: Demystifying authentication concepts in smartphones: ways and types to secure access. Mob. Inf. Syst. (Hindawi) **2018**, 16 (2018)
4. Finger snapping. https://en.wikipedia.org/wiki/Finger_snapping. Accessed 20 June 2018
5. About Face ID advanced technology. https://support.apple.com/en-us/HT208108. Accessed 20 June 2018
6. How the iPhone 5S Fingerprint Scanner Works and What It Means For You. https://gizmodo.com/how-the-iphone-5ss-fingerprint-scanner-works-and-what-1265703794. Accessed 20 June 2018
7. De Luca, A., Hang, A., Von Zezschwitz, E., Hussmann, H.: I feel like I'm taking selfies all day! Towards understanding biometric authentication on smartphones. In: 33rd Annual ACM Conference on Human Factors in Computing Systems, pp. 1411–1414 (2010)
8. Windows Hello face recognition spoofed with photographs. https://nakedsecurity.sophos.com/2018/01/02/windows-hello-face-recognition-spoofed-with-photographs/. Accessed 20 June 2018
9. iPhone 6 vulnerable to TouchID fingerprint hack. https://www.itnews.com.au/news/iphone-6-vulnerable-to-touchid-fingerprint-hack-392414. Accessed 20 June 2018
10. Hacker fakes German minister's fingerprints using photos of her hands. https://www.theguardian.com/technology/2014/dec/30/hacker-fakes-german-ministers-fingerprints-using-photos-of-her-hands. Accessed 20 June 2018
11. Buriro, A.: Behavioral biometrics for smartphone user authentication. Ph.D dissertation. University of Trento, Italy (2017)
12. Nguyen, T., Memon, N.: Smartwatches locking methods: a comparative study. In: Symposium on Usable Privacy and Security (SOUPS) (2017)
13. Lewis, A., Li, Y., Xie, M.: Real time motion-based authentication for smartwatch. In: IEEE Conference on Communications and Network Security (CNS), pp. 380–381 (2016)
14. Kumar, R., Phoha, V.V., Raina, R.: Authenticating users through their arm movement patterns. arXiv preprint arXiv:1603.02211 (2016)
15. Lu, C.X., Du, B., Kan, X., Wen, H., Markham, A., Trigoni, N.: VeriNet: user verification on smartwatches via behavior biometrics. In: Proceedings of the First ACM Workshop on Mobile Crowd sensing Systems and Applications, pp. 68–73 (2017)
16. Sitova, Z., et al.: HMOG: A New Biometric Modality for Continuous Authentication of Smartphone Users. arXiv preprint arXiv:1501.01199 (2015)
17. Buriro, A., Akhtar, Z., Crispo, B., Gupta, S.: Mobile biometrics: towards a comprehensive evaluation methodology. In: IEEE International Carnahan Conference on Security Technology (ICCST), pp. 1–6 (2017)
18. Buriro, A., Crispo, B., Delfrari, F., Wrona, K.: Hold and sign: a novel behavioral biometrics for smartphone user authentication. In: Proceedings of the IEEE Security and Privacy Workshops (SPW), pp. 276–285 (2016)

A Protocol to Strengthen
Password-Based Authentication

Itzel Vazquez Sandoval, Borce Stojkovski, and Gabriele Lenzini[✉]

SnT/University of Luxembourg, Luxembourg City, Luxembourg
{itzel.vazquezsandoval,borce.stojkovski,gabriele.lenzini}@uni.lu

Abstract. We discuss a password-based authentication protocol that we argue to be robust against password-guessing and off-line dictionary attacks. The core idea is to hash the passwords with a seed that comes from an OTP device, making the resulting identity token unpredictable for an adversary. We believe that the usability of this new protocol is the same as that of password-based methods with OTP, but has the advantage of not burdening users with having to choose strong passwords.

Keywords: Password-based authentication · Cryptographic protocols

1 Introduction

Password-based authentication is the most common mechanism for online authentication. It relies on one factor: 'something-you-know', and requests that the legitimate user proves knowledge of a username and a password. The whole security of the method rests, however, on the password, which must be kept secret and be chosen *strong i.e.*, unpredictable. Unfortunately, this is rarely happening.

Security research has extensively commented on the poor quality of people's choices regarding passwords (*e.g.*, see [2,7,10,11]). The problem is subtle. According to [9], people do have certain critical misunderstandings about what makes a password strong and are unaware of the complete attack surface, but their intuitions about what a secure password should look like are usually in line with password-cracking approaches. Despite that, their passwords are commonly short, built from predictable words and phrases which also tend to be semantically related, and are also often reused across different accounts. Regrettably, poor password management practices are also very common, which worsens the situation.

Weak passwords are particularly problematic. Hackers can easily guess them or they can steal password files, a common attack as recent news on the breaches

L. Gabriele—Authors are supported by the projects: pEp Security SA/SnT "Protocols for Privacy Security Analysis"; FNR-PRIDE "Security and Privacy for System Protection".

A. Saracino and P. Mori (Eds.): ETAA 2018, LNCS 11263, pp. 38–46, 2018.
https://doi.org/10.1007/978-3-030-04372-8_4

at Reddit[1], Twitter[2] and Yahoo![3] prove. Although login servers protectively store only the hash of the passwords, poorly chosen passwords are retrievable by off-line dictionary attacks. Attacks on password files are generally a preparation for further intrusions that take advantage of people's reuse of passwords.

This discussion raises an obvious *research question*: if we accept that users choose weak passwords, how can we guarantee that password-based authentication is secure *i.e.*, that it works with unpredictable identity tokens and with password files resilient to off-line dictionary attacks? And, if a solution exists, how can it be achieved without imposing too much burden on users? The goal of this short paper is to answer these questions, to propose a possible solution, and to discuss its security.

1.1 Scope of the Work

There might be several different ways to approach the above research questions and to find answers. Many researchers opt for supporting authentication without passwords (*e.g.*, see [8]); we are not interested in solutions of this kind since we intend to remain within the context of password-based authentication.

There are also methods that use tokens as alternative passwords, like those requesting freshly generated PINs. The security of such methods relies exclusively upon the possession of a personal device. We briefly comment on them in Sect. 4, mainly to compare their security with that of our solution, but using PINs and similar codes is not the answer we seek for our question.

So, what type of strategies remain in our scope? We see here at least two families of them. One includes techniques and resources that help users generate and memorize hard-to-guess passwords. They can be mnemonic strategies, but they cannot be taught to everyone and, we believe, the practice does not scale. Alternatively, they can be applications, such as the *password vaults* like Schneier's "Password Safe" or the compatible "Password Gorilla". They generate strong passwords on behalf of the user and keep them safe in an encrypted file on the user's personal device, available on demand. The drawback is that the vault's access is password-secured, which introduces a circular problem as the vault's access can be vulnerable to dictionary attacks. Besides, we are unaware of any research that brings evidence of a widespread adoption of password vaults, although their recent integration in some browsers will increase their use.

A second family includes protocols that implement second-factor authentication, and the second factor is often "something-you-have". Authentication is still password-based, but the identity of who is submitting a correct username and password is further verified by proving possession of a personal device (*e.g.*, a token generator, a phone, an account). To this family belongs a multitude of solutions (see for instance the Google 2-step verification[4]), but discussing each

---

[1] https://www.bbc.com/news/technology-45040804.
[2] http://www.wired.co.uk/article/twitter-hack-breach-32-million-passwords.
[3] https://www.nytimes.com/2016/12/14/technology/yahoo-hack.html.
[4] https://www.google.com/landing/2step/.

and every different instance in this quite crowded family is beyond the ambition of this paper. We can, however, observe one important fact: while the trustworthiness of a user's authentication is strengthened by the second factor, users can still choose weak passwords and the leak of a password file remains a serious issue.

Nevertheless, it is in this category that we find our main source of inspiration. In particular, we look at protocols where the second factor is a One-Time-Password (OTP) device. Such protocols are common, and the closest to the password-based ones in terms of usability: in addition to the username and password, they require the user to input also a nonce which will be submitted simultaneously.

1.2 Previous Work and Contribution

To the best of our knowledge, the protocol that we describe here is novel, but the motivation of the work is rooted in previous research of ours [4].

There, we studied a password-based authentication system first described by Jewels and Rivest [5]. Its main goal is to make the stealing of a password file *tamper-evident*. The system, called *honeywords system*, has a simple security working principle: legitimate user-chosen passwords are stored together with some decoy words, called honeywords, which are indistinguishable from the password (*e.g.*, indistinguishable as "whitemoon" is from "redsun"). An adversary who stole the password file and retrieved the words by an off-line dictionary attack cannot do better than picking one word at random, revealing that the file has been leaked if he tries to authenticate with a wrongly picked word.

In [4] we reviewed the protocol to make it tamper-evident when the Login Server (LS)'s code is corrupted by the adversary. The resulting protocol seems to suggest a completely new way to authenticate users, which also makes a password file resilient to off-line dictionary attacks. We left for future work to look into the matter; here we develop that idea into a novel password-based authentication protocol.

We anticipate that our solution spares users from having to choose strong passwords provided that they use an OTP device. But, differently from the common use of the device as a proof-of-possession, we use OTP's numbers to generate fresh identification tokens with high entropy, that depend on the password; they are unpredictable (by an adversary) and not vulnerable to dictionary attacks.

2 An Enhanced Password-Based Authentication

We assume two roles: the User (U) and a LS. We envision three different protocols: registration, authentication, and update.

Assumptions. We assume that U and LS communicate through a secure channel *e.g.*, implemented by a TLS protocol. We also assume that a pre-image resistant hashing algorithm H, such as SHA-512, is applied to passwords and that LS stores hashed passwords as usual. We omit obvious checks like verifying that the username exists. As well, we assume that U holds an OTP device which has been delivered securely, as it is usually the case. The device's output, which changes every time the device is operated, is aligned with the output produced by a corresponding OTP's generator algorithm in the LS. $OTP(n)$ is the number produced by the device when used for the n-th time (equivalently, n times).

Registration. U follows this protocol to register to a service and to set his password w (see Fig. 1). U operates the OTP device for the first time to get a number, $OTP(1)$ (**1**). The password is hashed using H and then rehashed, this time using $OTP(1)$ as a seed. The token obtained, $h^{r_1}(H(w))$ is sent to LS together with U's id, u (**2**). On reception, LS anticipates the next OTP number, $r_2 = OTP(2)$ (by operating the device twice) and rehashes the identity token it has received from U using that number (**3,4**). LS relies on a strategy that we describe next and that does not require LS to know the password. The rehashed token, once more hashed with H, is stored as u's password (**5**). LS also stores r_2 and the registration for U concludes (**6**). Note that here we have assumed that the OTP generates a new number each time it is used. If instead the output of the device depended on the current time, as some OTP systems work, the protocol would have to be modified. This is not a dramatic change, but for space reasons we omit that version.

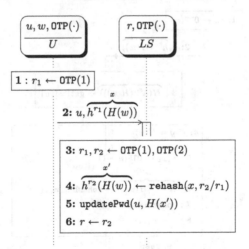

Fig. 1. Registration

The hashing is implemented by *cryptographic exponentiation*. For each user id u, LS possesses g_u, a generator of a multiplicative subgroup $\mathbb{G}$ of order q. Then,

u's hashed password, $H(w)$, is re-hashed using g_u^r, where $r \in \{1, \cdots, q-1\}$ is a random number. Herein r is obtained by operating the OTP device. The value submitted for authentication is $g_u^{r \cdot H(w)}$, which we denote as $h^r(H(w))$ to stress that it is a hashing and to lighten the notation regarding u's dependency. Using this scheme LS can, for another $r' \in \{1, \cdots, q-1\}$, calculate $h^{r'}(H(w))$ from $h^r(H(w))$ only by knowing r and r' and not $H(w)$. In fact:

$$h^{r'}(H(w)) = g_u^{r' \cdot H(w)} = g_u^{r \cdot \frac{r'}{r} \cdot H(w)} = (g_u^{r \cdot H(w)})^{\frac{r'}{r}} = h^r(H(w))^{\frac{r'}{r}} \qquad (1)$$

Such a feature is at the core of the authentication procedure.

Authentication. The protocol's sequence of messages, for a general authentication round n, is shown in Fig. 2. U submits a username u, and a token that is the password w, hashed with H and rehashed with the current $\mathtt{OTP}(n)$ (**2**). LS retrieves u's token from the password file (**3**) and proceeds with authenticating U. For this, it hashes the received token x, which must match the token y stored in the file (**4**). If the check succeeds, LS uses the OTP to anticipate the next number and calculates the next identity token of u (**5,6**) by using the rehashing as described in Eq. (1) above; then LS updates the password file and r (**7,8**); otherwise, the access is denied. U receives a response (**9**).

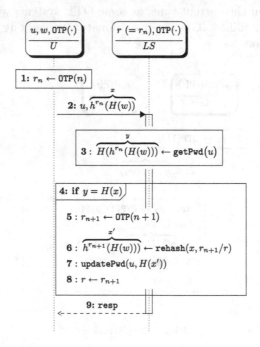

Fig. 2. The n-th ($n > 1$) run of the authentication protocol

Update. The update protocol allows U to change the password. It combines authentication and registration. We omit the full description for reasons of space.

2.1   Security Analysis

We discuss the security of the protocol in reference to an adversary that either (a) tries to guess U's password, or (b) has eavesdropped U's communication, or (c) has stolen the password file and tries off-line dictionary attacks on it, or (d) has stolen the OTP device and the password file (but not the password).

At the end of round n of the authentication, the value stored by LS is $H(h^{r_{n+1}}(H(w)))$, where H is the common hashing. Since we allow the user to choose the password, we cannot exclude the possibility of w being weak and thus of the intruder guessing it. However, without holding the OTP device the intruder cannot generate the right identity token to get access, nor use LS as an oracle to verify whether the guess is correct. This answers case (a).

Even if the intruder could observe the communication and retrieve one identity token $h^x(w)$ from any previous sessions of any protocol, he cannot reuse that token: identity tokens are one-time valid. Neither can the intruder guess the new token. If we work under CDH assumption, the knowledge of previous identity tokens of the form $h^r(x)$ for some r, does not give any advantage to the attacker even if he combines this knowledge with the password. To generate the next identity token the adversary needs also the OTP number generated by the device. This answers case (b).

Getting possession of the password file does not help the intruder either. First, since the re-hashing is not directly applied to plain text words, but to $H(w)$, the values obtained by the re-hashing function seeded with the OTP number are not retrievable by a dictionary attack. Second, he would need to calculate H's pre-image to extract from the password file the next u's token, but this is not possible since H is pre-image resistant. This answers case (c).

Finally, if the attacker were able to obtain the OTP and the password file, but not the password, he still could not authenticate. Even in the very unrealistic situation where the attacker knows g and the stored LS's r, he cannot generate any next u's identity tokens because he would need H's pre-image for that, *i.e.*, $h^r(H(w))$ which is hashed in the password file. Just for the sake of speculation, we comment that there might exist one remote possibility for the attacker to be able to launch an off-line dictionary attack: steal an OTP ready to be used for the $n+1$ time and get a password file that contains exactly $H(h^{r_{n+1}}(H(w)))$. But the intruder cannot know whether he finds himself in this lucky situation.

Aiming to formally prove our claims, we analyzed the protocols in Proverif [1]; the results confirm that access to the system is granted only when there has been a request from a user and the hash of the credentials submitted (user-id, password and OTP number) corresponds to the value stored in the password file owned by the LS. In this short paper we omit the part where we describe the analysis and the code, but we plan to add it in an extended version of the paper.

3   Implementation

The most obvious way to implement the protocol's main operation, exponentiation, is by elliptic curve (EC) multiplication. To protect implementations against remote timing attacks [3], the time-cost of the multiplication is usually t_c, a constant that depends on the chosen curve c. Thus, the time-cost of our protocol's implementation is constant in t_c. We do not have measures over our protocol performances (we are currently implementing our solution in C# atop the Microsoft .NET framework), but from previous experiences with more complex protocols using exponentiation, as the one documented in [4], we expect the overhead on the user and on the login server to be negligible.

In a practical implementation, we have to consider that a user can accidentally burn some OTP numbers. This problem can be solved by the LS anticipating the next, let us say m, OTPs. Thus, LS has to store for each user a row of values, disposing of the old ones when a valid token is presented.

4   Discussion, Related Work, and Future Work

Our protocol has two main advantages: (1) it releases users from the burden of having to choose strong passwords at the price of handling an OTP device and of minor changes in implementation of the authentication protocol; (2) it makes it less interesting for adversaries to hack the password file, since they cannot use it for further attacks neither in the same nor in other domains.

In proposing our solution we were resolved to keep the use of passwords, which is still the mostly used method for authentication. In current commercial applications, comparable solutions are, however, available. More and more services request users to submit one-time PINs which are generated on (or sent to) their personal devices. The PINs are submitted instead of the password. Other services welcome innovative dongles, like the YubiKey[5], multi-purpose security tokens that can store passwords, generate OTPs, and can play different challenge-response protocols. A formal analysis of the security of such alternative solutions is future work, but, at least informally, it seems that their security is equivalent to that of our protocol: they do not handle tokens that are vulnerable to guess and off-line dictionary attacks. If there is a factor that can make a difference, it is the usability aspect, since the ceremonies and the interfaces that they implement for the authentication differ from one another. We leave for future work to define research questions and to design experiments apt to measure usable security aspects for such a diversified set of authentication procedures.

The closest theoretical work to ours, is that of Lamport [6]. In short, it demands that, at the nth round, LS stores a $(K - n)$-time nested hash of the password while the user authenticates by providing a token that is a $(K - n - 1)$-time nested hash of it. Here, K is a shared constant. Lamport's protocol ensures the same advantages (1) and (2) because LS stores a token whose pre-image, if

---

[5] https://www.yubico.com/.

stolen, cannot be calculated. At the same time LS can efficiently perform the authentication check. Lamport's and our solution do probably differ at the level of usability and performance, but we have not made any measurements yet.

Limitation. We wrote this short paper primarily to share our idea and to open a discussion on it. Since the intuition behind our solution originates from a research we did while addressing another problem (see Sect. 1.2), we branched from that work and started with the protocol design without having done first an extensive comparison with the state-of-the-art. Thus, although the research reported herein is original (*i.e.*, not published elsewhere) our related work section is limited to a few commercial protocols that use passwords or similar tokens; it lacks consideration of other theoretical ideas that may be close to what we have conceived. The only exception is the Lamport's authentication protocol [6]. Published in 1981, the work has been suggested to us by a reviewer, to whom we are grateful. An extensive comparative analysis of the two protocols in terms of security, performance, and usability is also left for future work.

References

1. Blanchet, B., Smyth, B., Cheval, V.: ProVerif 1.96: Automatic Cryptographic Protocol Verifier, User Manual and Tutorial (2016)
2. Bonneau, J.: The science of guessing: analyzing an anonymized corpus of 70 million passwords. In: 2012 IEEE Symposium on Security and Privacy (SP), pp. 538–552. IEEE (2012)
3. Brumley, B.B., Tuveri, N.: Remote timing attacks are still practical. In: Atluri, V., Diaz, C. (eds.) ESORICS 2011. LNCS, vol. 6879, pp. 355–371. Springer, Heidelberg (2011). https://doi.org/10.1007/978-3-642-23822-2_20
4. Genç, Z.A., Lenzini, G., Ryan, P.Y.A., Vázquez Sandoval, I.: A security analysis, and a fix, of a code-corrupted honeywords system. In: Proceedings of the 4th International Conference on Information Systems Security and Privacy (ICISSP 2018), pp. 83–95 (2018)
5. Juels, A., Rivest, R.L.: Honeywords: making password-cracking detectable. In: Proceedings of the 2013 ACM SIGSAC Conference on Computer & Communications Security, pp. 145–160. ACM (2013)
6. Lamport, L.: Password authentication with insecure communication. Commun. ACM **24**(11), 770–772 (1981)
7. Malone, D., Maher, K.: Investigating the distribution of password choices. In: Proceedings of the 21st International Conference on World Wide Web, WWW 2012, pp. 301–310. ACM, New York (2012)
8. Stajano, F.: Pico: no more passwords!. In: Christianson, B., Crispo, B., Malcolm, J., Stajano, F. (eds.) Security Protocols 2011. LNCS, vol. 7114, pp. 49–81. Springer, Heidelberg (2011). https://doi.org/10.1007/978-3-642-25867-1_6
9. Ur, B., Bees, J., Segreti, S.M., Bauer, L., Christin, N., Cranor, L.F.: Do users' perceptions of password security match reality? In: Proceedings of the 2016 CHI Conference on Human Factors in Computing Systems (CHI 2016), pp. 3748–3760 (2016)

10. von Zezschwitz, E., De Luca, A., Hussmann, H.: Survival of the shortest: a retrospective analysis of influencing factors on password composition. In: Kotzé, P., Marsden, G., Lindgaard, G., Wesson, J., Winckler, M. (eds.) INTERACT 2013. LNCS, vol. 8119, pp. 460–467. Springer, Heidelberg (2013). https://doi.org/10.1007/978-3-642-40477-1_28
11. Wash, R., Rader, E., Berman, R., Wellmer, Z.: Understanding password choices: how frequently entered passwords are re-used across websites. In: Proceedings of 12th Symposium on Usable Privacy and Security (SOUPS 2016), pp. 175–188. USENIX Association, Denver, CO (2016)

Managing Private Credentials by Privacy-Preserving Biometrics

Bian Yang[✉] and Guoqiang Li

Norwegian University of Science and Technology (NTNU),
2815 Gjøvik, Norway
{bian.yang, guoqiang.li}@ntnu.no

Abstract. We investigate in this paper the need to managing a user's private credentials using privacy-preserving biometrics, define several private credential management work models under different trust models between a user and an external party. A general pipeline using privacy-preserving biometrics for private credential management is proposed to achieve the purpose of biometric template protection, biometric-secret binding, and biometric recognition accuracy performance improvement. The proposed scheme was implemented and tested in the European CIP project PIDaaS, and demonstrated advantages in privacy preservation and accuracy performance preservation.

Keywords: Private identity · Privacy-preserving biometrics
Biometric template protection · Biometric-secret binding
User-centric identity management

1 Introduction

An identity authentication mechanism enables a service provider to distinguish their customers and customize the service for each of them. However, in most services, managing users identities increases the business operational burden and also the risk of data leakage. As the GDPR strengthens the data subjects' rights to their personal data and specifies the penalty on data breach, service providers can be motivated to outsource customer identity management to a professional party in order to reduce the risk of data breach. Identity management outsourcing models can include identity federation and Single-Sign-On (SSO) (*e.g.*, the Google Identity Platform [1] and the Facebook Login [2]), a cross-service identity platform (*e.g.*, OpenID [3] and bankID [4]), and claimed-based identity management schemes [5, 6].

While service providers have many options (as mentioned above) to outsource the identity management task, users usually have to manage (memorize, take a note, save a file, *etc.*) by themselves their identities for authentication (*e.g.*, account name, identification number, password, PIN, private key, *etc.*) – called "private credential" in this paper. As there are increasing private credentials for an ordinary user to manage, the user has a growing need to outsource credentials' management to a professional party. This party can be either a software such as a password manager, or an organization delegated to compute in an authentication protocol. A password manager with a master user account and secret is for instance a typical way to manage credentials.

© Springer Nature Switzerland AG 2018
A. Saracino and P. Mori (Eds.): ETAA 2018, LNCS 11263, pp. 47–55, 2018.
https://doi.org/10.1007/978-3-030-04372-8_5

When it comes to the possibility using biometrics to replace a master password to manage a credential manager [7], the configuration for outsourcing to a private credential manager (PCM) can be complicated. Using biometrics implies processing the biometric sample, extracting and protecting the derived feature, and securely storing the generated biometric template. All these burden a user in terms of computation and security. In addition, the user may still need to manage a master secret (*e.g.*, a master password to the PCM, a secret key for generating a protected template, *etc.*), or other supplementary data (SD) that could be needed in operating a PCM. The ISO/IEC JTC1 24745 on Biometric Information Protection [8] presented a general model for processing a plain biometric feature b and generating a protected template (PT), which includes a pseudonymous identifier (PI) for direct comparison and an auxiliary data (AD) for reconstructing a new PI for comparison. What data out of $\{b, SD, PI, AD\}$ and the associated computations can be delegated to a PCM may depend on various considerations (*e.g.*, efficiency, reliability, cost, security, trust model, law compliance, *etc.*) among which the trust model can be decisive.

One noticeable step towards the concept of biometrics-enabled private credential management was made by the FIDO alliance [9], whose UAF standard provides a general way to binding and unlocking a service-specific private key for authenticating the user to a service provider via the FIDO Authenticator placed in the device. The drawbacks of the FIDO solution include (1) it is a device-centric solution, *i.e.*, the service-specific private key is generated per service provider, per device, and per user account, and the biometric verification takes place at the device. Upon a device loss a user has to revoke the certificate and the private key associated with the lost device, and create a new registration including enrolling her/his biometrics on the new device. This implies hardly any portability, which is not compatible with the concept of the claimed-based identity management. (2) it is not specified in FIDO UAF how a biometric template is stored and how a service-specific private key can be unlocked from a biometric verification. The security in storing the biometric template and the private key depends highly on the device's hardware and software environment for protecting these data. The variance in devices and FIDO UAF authenticator's implementation increases the complexity of configuring data protection on a specific device.

Instead of following the device-centric concept, we propose in this paper a user-centric approach to managing private credentials by privacy-preserving biometrics. In Sect. 2, we propose three typical work modes in which a biometric private credential manager (PCM) can be configured to manage credentials. In Sect. 3, we propose a privacy-preserving biometric-secret binding scheme. Section 4 gives the performance testing results of the proposed scheme, and Sect. 5 concludes this paper.

2 Configuring a Biometric Private Credential Manager

We denote in this paper the service provider as SP, a user who wants to authenticate her/him with a SP as User, and the identity provider as IdP. The identity data held and managed by a User for authentication is a Credential, and the data held and managed by an IdP or a SP to attest and ascertain the User's identity claim is a Registry. A SP can outsource the identity authentication computation or even decision making to an IdP as a party trusted by the SP, which is always assumed in this paper. Similarly, a User may reply solely on a software (or with hardware additionally) denoted as a Private Credential Manager Client (PCMC) for managing their credentials, or outsource data storage and part of computation required for authentication to an independent party denoted as a Private Credential Manager Server (PCMS). From a User's perspective, how to configure the data {biometric feature b, supplementary data SD, pseudonymous identifier PI, auxiliary data AD} (explained in Sect. 1) and the associated computations among different parties can be varied.

One decisive factor is how much trust a User has on PCMS so that (s)he can decide whether to outsource to PCMS the storage of AD (*e.g.*, a protected biometric template), or instead, the storage, part of template generation computation, and even the cryptographic authentication process interacted with IdP. We define the following three work modes of a PCM based on a User' different levels of trust on a PCMS. Note that the defined work modes do not represent all possible configurations among the parties. Instead, they are assumed the typical ones from the User perspective.

Work Mode I (local computation and storage): as showed in Fig. 1(a), the User relies solely on the PCMC to take as input b, SD_1 (*e.g.*, a master password or PIN), and SD_2 (*e.g.*, a salt managed by IdP), and generate and store AD locally on the User's device. Together with AD is generated PI which can be used as the secret for a cryptographic authentication protocol between PCMC and IdP. This work mode can be deemed as a biometric version of a local password manager or a FIDO UAF authenticator. The User has to fully trust her/his device and software on it.

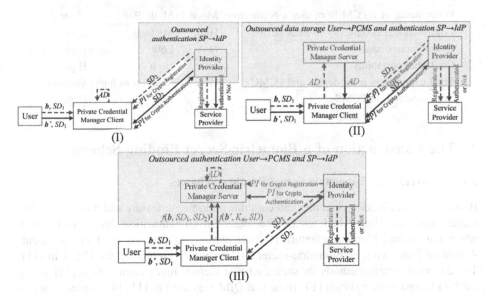

Fig. 1. Work modes for a biometric private credential manager

Work Mode II (local computation and outsourced storage): as showed in Fig. 1(b), the User relies on the PCMC to take as input b, SD_1, and SD_2, and generate AD. The

AD is stored in PCMS and will be retrieved by PCMC for generating a new *PI* used as the secret for a cryptographic authentication between PCMC and IdP. This work mode outsources the storage of *AD* to PCMS, and therefore the User has to trust the PCMS on its capacity of properly protecting an *AD* from leakage if this *AD* should be kept confidential. Otherwise the User should use encryption or a biometric template protection scheme [10] to ensure *AD* does not reveal any information about b.

Work Mode III (distributed computation and outsourced storage): as showed in Fig. 1(c), the User relies on the PCMC to take as input b, SD_1, and SD_2. Instead of generating *AD* directly, the PCMC can perform a lightweight protection $f(b, SD_1, SD_2)$ on b and send the partially protected b to PCMS. Then the PCMS will continue the biometric feature protection, verification, and the cryptographic authentication with IdP. Splitting up the work effort between PCMC and PCMS can ensure that (1) PCMC's computational workload be shared by PCMS, when PCMC is operated on a power-constrained mobile device; (2) PCMS provide better protection for *AD* and *PI* when for any reasons the PCMS is more trusted than the PCMC; (3) PCMC provide an extra layer of protection for b when the PCMS is not fully trusted.

Table 1 summarizes the three work modes qualitatively evaluated in different criteria. The proposed privacy-preserving scheme in Sect. 3 can make the most of the Work Mode III when both storage and part of computation are outsourced to a less trusted party as PCMS.

Table 1. Comparison among work modes of a private credential manager.

Performance of a PCM from user's perspective	Mode I	Mode II	Mode III
Computational complexity in local device	High	Medium	Low
Cost in outsourcing	N/A	Low	High
Credential portability	Low	High	High
Trust required on local device and PCMC	High	Medium to high	Medium
Trust required on PCMS	N/A	Low	High

3   The Construction of a Biometric-Secret Binding Scheme

3.1   Conventional Biometric-Secret Binding Schemes

Biometric-secret binding schemes can combine a biometric feature and a cryptographic secret during enrolment and release the secret for authentication during verification when the probed biometric feature is close enough to the one used in enrolment. A general framework of biometric-secret binding was presented in the Fig. 1 in [11]. Typical construction methods for such a scheme include fuzzy commitment [12], fuzzy vault [13], and secure sketch [14] (note that QIM was used in [11, 14] to encode secret bits by choosing quantizers, which should be distinguished from the other type of secure sketch [15, 16] which generates secret bits from biometric features). Due to lack of effective feature processing steps, such biometric-secret binding schemes are known for their distinct biometric recognition accuracy degradation.

Unlike conventional fuzzy commitment schemes with compromised biometric recognition accuracy and the security concern of key-inversion (*i.e.*, deriving plain biometric feature from the leaked secret), we propose in Sect. 3.2 a new feature transformation with dimension-expanded/reduced random projection and reliable dimensions selection in order to (1) preserve the biometric recognition accuracy; (2) enhance the protection of the biometric information beyond that of the secret so that an key-inversion attack will hardly work; and (3) shield the plain biometric feature securely from a delegated authentication operator (*e.g.*, the PCMS) in Work Mode III.

3.2   The Proposed Privacy-Preserving Biometric-Secret Binding Scheme

The proposed privacy-preserving biometric-secret binding scheme consists of four steps in sequence: random projection, reliable dimensions selection, binarization, and fuzzy commitment. Suppose a User possesses her/his biometric feature vector b, the supplementary data SD (including both SD_1 under her/his control and SD_2 which can be retrieved from IdP upon a request from the User), and a secret S for binding.

Enrolment:

Step 1: Dimension-Reduced and/or Expanded Random Projection. Each b can be transformed to a vector pv via random projection which largely preserves the distance. A random projection can be a dimension-reduced one (*i.e.*, a surjection) so that b is hard to precisely recover from pv due to information loss. This distance-preserving property makes random projection an attractive solution [17] to biometric template protection. Random projection can be also used to expand the dimension of b in order to obtain better biometric comparison accuracy [18, 19] when using simple quantization (*e.g.*, thresholding by sign) to binarize pv. The dimension-reduced and the dimension-expanded random projections can be also used in tandem in order to achieve both privacy protection (irreversibility defined in [20]) for b and maximized recognition accuracy from pv. In practice, it can be at the User's decision either or both of the two can be adopted in the proposed pipeline, depending on the need of the trust on the outsourced PCMS or the recognition accuracy performance. **Step 2: Reliable Dimensions Selection.** The expanded random projection provides a rich set of projected dimensions among which the most reliable dimensions can be selected to construct a vector rv as a reliable representation of b. The reliability can be defined in the sense that a dimension rv_i ($1 \leq i \leq N$, where N is the dimension of pv) has an as-small-as-possible intra-class distance (from an expectation value of rv_i of samples from the same biometric characteristic) while an as-large-as-possible inter-class distance (from the same dimension of other users). In practice, multiple samples are needed from the same biometric characteristic to estimate the expectation value in each dimension, which can be done during enrolment. A separate dataset is needed to form an "imposter set" to calculate the inter-class distances between an enrolled rv and those projected vectors generated from the imposter set. To rank all the dimensions rv_i ($1 \leq i \leq N$) in reliability, simple metrics such as Equal Error Rate can be adopted to measure the dis-similarity of the two distance sets' distribution. The indices of the selected dimensions are saved as AD_1 locally (Work Mode I) or in PCMS (Work Mode II and III). **Step 3: Binarization.** A binarization step follows the reliable dimensions selection in order to convert the selected reliable dimensions (*i.e.* vector rv) to a binary representation, denoted as a vector bv, to be used for the next step of secret binding. A binarization method (*e.g.*, simple thresholding by mean value or sign, or a unary representation) can generate a vector that is suitable for Hamming distance calculation, implying that all generated binary bits should be approximately equally weighted and distributed. **Step 4: Secret Binding - Fuzzy Commitment.** Assuming a secret S (*e.g.*, password or a private key) has been created for a cryptographic authentication protocol between the User (PCMC/PCMS) and the IdP, we can use a secret binding scheme to combine S and bv into an AD_2 stored locally (Work Mode I) or in PCMS (Work Mode II and III). We use the fuzzy commitment scheme [12] to achieve this purpose. This enrolment process takes as input $\{b, SD_1, SD_2, S\}$ and outputs the protected template $\{AD_1, AD_2\}$, whose breach would have only limited risk in privacy breach regarding b, if not all three data $\{SD_1, SD_2, S\}$ are leaked.

Verification:

Step 1: Dimension-Reduced and/or Expanded Random Projection. During verification, a biometric feature vector b' together with $\{SD_1, SD_2\}$ is input to the pipeline, and the step is exactly same as the Step 1 during enrolment. **Step 2: Reliable Dimensions Selection.** The saved AD_1 recording selected indices is retrieved and supplied to the projected vector pv' derived from b' to form a rv' as a reliable representation of b'. **Step 3: Binarization.** The same method as in enrolment is used to obtain a binary representation vector bv' from rv'. **Step 4: Secret Releasing - Fuzzy Commitment.** Via the secret releasing step in fuzzy commitment, an error-correction decoded result S' is released for the subsequent cryptographic authentication protocol.

Depending on the trust a User has on an independent PCMS, the User can choose to complete the Step 1–4 in the three different work modes. In the Work Mode I, all the 4 steps are completed in the local device (PCMC) that is fit for the scenario where the User has low trust level on an external party besides IdP. In the Work Mode II and III, the User has medium and high trust on a PCMS respectively, and therefore storage and even part of computation in protected template generation can be outsourced to a PCMS. Figure 2(a) and (b) show the pipeline described above in the Work Mode II and III respectively with different steps and data managed by different parties. The underlying rationale for the difference is that a User may add an extra protection, in addition to fuzzy commitment, for b via a dimension-reduced random projection step prior to sending b to PCMS. The stored protected biometric template $\{AD_1, AD_2\}$ can be safely stored locally or outsourced with little concern in privacy leakage of b. Via changing the random matrix for projecting b and the secret S used by fuzzy commitment, unlinkable $\{AD_1, AD_2\}$ can be derived from the same biometric characteristic.

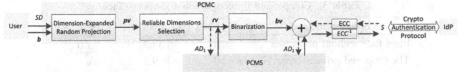

(a)   Work Mode II: outsourced identity data storage

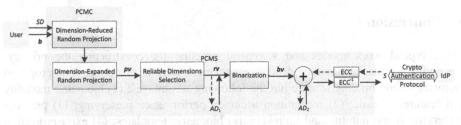

(b) Work Mode III: outsourced authentication

Fig. 2. Proposed privacy-preserving biometric-secret binding pipeline in Work Mode II and III

4   Performance Testing

We tested the proposed scheme in the pilots developed under the EU-CIP project PIDaaS (www.pidaas.eu). Two biometric modalities – face and voice – with the COTS SDK from Viulib [21] and Alize [22] respectively, were adopted in the pilots. Both SDKs generate fixed-length plain biometric feature vector b. In total 47 participants contributed to the test datasets. 3 face samples were used for enrolment and generating AD_1, and another 34 face samples were used as probes. 5 voice samples (in each sample a random set of 5 digits were spoken) with/without environmental noises were used for enrolment and generating AD_1, and another 6 voice samples were used as probes. If a probe vector is sufficiently close to the enrolled vector, the secret S could be successfully released. As the authentication conclusion is binary, we got only one performance point in terms of False Match Rate (FMR) and False Non-Match Rate (FNMR) instead of a continuous Detection Error Tradeoff curve or an Equal Error Rate (EER). The performance reported here from voice recognition were generated from the "imposter scenario" where all feature vectors included in inter-class distance calculation were derived from the same set of 5 digits spoken. Table 2 presents the performance from two representative sets of 5 digits, and Table 3 presents the performance from the face case. Though the accuracy performances were calculated from small-scale datasets, we observed that the biometric probes can be matched with well-preserved accuracy universally. The non-degradation in performance could be attributed to the dimension-expanded random projection and the reliable dimension selection steps that made the most of biometric features.

Table 2. Comparison in recognition accuracy – voice with 2 different sets of 5 digits spoken

Voice recognition method	FMR (%)	FNMR (%)	EER (%)
Plain voice without protection	0/0	2.4/9.5	0.2/1.2
The proposed privacy-preserving voice	0/0	3.5/5.9	n/a/

Table 3. Comparison in recognition accuracy – face

Face recognition method	FMR (%)	FNMR (%)	EER (%)
Plain face without protection	0	33.3	1.0
The proposed privacy-preserving face	0	9.3	n/a

5 Conclusion

Three typical work modes and a general pipeline for constructing the privacy-preserving biometrics based credential management were in this paper. The proposed biometric-secret binding scheme has the following advantages: (1) biometric modality and feature agnostic; (2) recognition accuracy performance preserving; (3) privacy-preserving (irreversibility and unlinkability) biometric templates; (4) extra protection for the biometric information when the authentication function is outsourced.

References

1. Google Identity Platform. https://developers.google.com/identity/
2. Facebook Login. https://developers.facebook.com/docs/facebook-login/
3. OpenID. https://zh.wikipedia.org/wiki/OpenID
4. bankID. https://www.bankid.no/en/company/
5. Claim-Based Identity. https://en.wikipedia.org/wiki/Claims-based_identity
6. Alrodhan, W., Mitchell, C.: Enhancing user authentication in claim-based identity management. In: 2010 International Symposium on Collaborative Technologies and Systems, pp. 75–83 (2010)
7. Yang, B., Chu, H., Li, G., Petrovic, S., Busch, C.: Cloud password manager using privacy-preserved biometrics. In: Proceedings of 2014 IEEE International Conference on Cloud Engineering (2014)
8. ISO/IEC 24745: Biometric information protection (2011)
9. FIDO Alliance. https://fidoalliance.org/
10. Nandakumar, K., Jain, A.: Biometric template protection: bridging the performance gap between theory and practice. IEEE Sig. Process. Mag. **32**(5), 88–100 (2015)
11. Bui, F., Martin, K., Lu, H., Plataniotis, K., Hatzinakos, D.: Fuzzy key binding strategies based on quantization index modulation (QIM) for biometric encryption (BE) applications. IEEE Trans. Inf. Forensics Secur. **5**(1), 118–132 (2010)
12. Juels, A., Wattenberg, M.: A fuzzy commitment scheme. In: Proceedings of the 6th ACM Conference on Computer and Communications Security, pp. 28–36 (1999)
13. Juels, A., Sudan, M.: A fuzzy vault scheme. Des. Codes Crypto. **38**(2), 237–257 (2006)
14. Buhan, I., Doumen, J., Hartel, P., Veldhuis, R.: Constructing practical fuzzy extractors using QIM centre for telematics and information technology. University of Twente, Enschede, Technical report. TR-CTIT-07-52, pp. 1381-3625 (2007)
15. Sutcu, Y., Li, Q., Memon, N.: Protecting biometric templates with sketch: theory and practice. IEEE Trans. Inf. Forensics Secur. **2**(3), 503–512 (2007)
16. Dodis, Y., Ostrovsky, R., Reyzin, L., Smith, A.: Fuzzy extractors: how to generate strong keys from biometrics and other noisy data. SIAM J. Comp. **38**(1), 97–139 (2008)

17. Teoh, A., Ngo, D., Goh, A.: Biohashing: two factor authentication featuring fingerprint data and tokenised random number. Pattern Recogn. **37**(11), 2245–2255 (2004)
18. Yang, B., Busch, C., Gafurov, D., Bours, P.: Renewable minutiae templates with tunable size and security. In: ICPR, pp. 878–881 (2010)
19. Yang, B., Hartung, D., Simoens, K., Busch, C.: Dynamic random projection for biometric template protection. In: IEEE BTAS, pp. 1–7 (2010)
20. Simoens, K., et al.: Criteria towards metrics for benchmarking template protection algorithms. In: ICB (2012)
21. http://www.viulib.org
22. https://github.com/ALIZE-Speaker-Recognition

Policy Support for Autonomous Swarms of Drones

Alan Cullen[1], Erisa Karafili[2(✉)], Alan Pilgrim[1], Chris Williams[3], and Emil Lupu[2]

[1] BAE Systems Applied Intelligence Laboratories, Great Baddow, UK
alan.pilgrim@baesystems.com
[2] Imperial College London, London, UK
{e.karafili,e.c.lupu}@imperial.ac.uk
[3] Defence Scientific and Technology Laboratory, London, UK
cwilliams@dstl.gov.uk

Abstract. In recent years drones have become more widely used in military and non-military applications. Automation of these drones will become more important as their use increases. Individual drones acting autonomously will be able to achieve some tasks, but swarms of autonomous drones working together will be able to achieve much more complex tasks and be able to better adapt to changing environments. In this paper we describe an example scenario involving a swarm of drones from a military coalition and civil/humanitarian organisations that are working collaboratively to monitor areas at risk of flooding. We provide a definition of a swarm and how they can operate by exchanging messages. We define a flexible set of policies that are applicable to our scenario that can be easily extended to other scenarios or policy paradigms. These policies ensure that the swarms of drones behave as expected (e.g., for safety and security). Finally we discuss the challenges and limitations around policies for autonomous swarms and how new research, such as generative policies, can aid in solving these limitations.

Keywords: Swarm · Drone systems · Policies · Coalitions

1 Introduction

Drones are being adopted in dull, dirty and dangerous military operations [15] as well as non-military applications such as pipeline inspection, highway monitoring and filming [11]. As drones become accepted and more capable there is emerging interest in the potential of swarms of multiple cooperating drones.

In this work we provide a definition for a swarm of drones. Through the use of a scenario we describe how the drones of a swarm communicate and coordinate with each other to achieve their common and individual goals. The constraints and rules of the swarm are represented using a generic policy language, as a set of policies that regulate the actions and behaviours of the drones of a swarm.

© Springer Nature Switzerland AG 2018
A. Saracino and P. Mori (Eds.): ETAA 2018, LNCS 11263, pp. 56–70, 2018.
https://doi.org/10.1007/978-3-030-04372-8_6

There is increasing interest over the swarm of drones as they rise in popularity and use. DARPA carried out a *capture the flag* trial between opposing teams, each flying dozens of low cost drones, demonstrating both robustness in numbers and the benefits of diversity between fixed wing and quadcopter platforms [1]. Another swarming example is provided by a simulation of data ferrying (i.e. physically transporting data between communicating parties) using drones where policies are used to synchronize the flight of drones that cannot communicate directly with each other [13]. Swarms are a familiar concept in nature, described by collective nouns such as a swarm of insects, a flock of birds, or a school of fish. These swarms have benefits such as protection from predators and a larger effective search pattern in the quest for food [25].

The scenario we introduce in our work commences with a requirement for four drones to observe seven surveillance targets. It is reasonable to assert that in this situation an optimal allocation of drones to specific targets will outperform flocking solutions - where the drones move together in a crowd from one surveillance target to another. The exception is possibly when the probability of attack is so high that the defensive benefits of flocking outweigh a solution that, for example, maximizes the observation time at each target. This is not surprising because surveillance and search have different requirements, and even if drones are deployed on a search mission they may benefit by exploiting capabilities lacking in nature such as long range communications.

A swarm can comprise a number of different components and resources. The swarm needs to make decisions about the tasks to perform, where to fly, as well as to coordinate with the other components during the flight and to communicate with other components or the leader of the swarm. This decision process is made depending on the constraints and rules already defined to the swarm, as well as the environmental/mission conditions where the swarm is operating. In our work we introduce a set of policies that represents these constraints and rules and are used by the swarm decision process.

1.1 Related Work

Lately, research focused on unmanned aircrafts (e.g., drone systems) is increasing, especially with the expansion of their usage (e.g., drone package delivery like *Amazon's Prime Air* [2] or *Google's Project Wing* [29]). Different studies have been made by Amazon [3,4], Google [14] and NASA [23] concerning the safety and efficiency of design, management, operations of unmanned aircraft systems (UAS), their safe airspace access, and their communications and collaborations. The authors in [12] present a model of architecture for coordinating the access of UAS to controlled airspace and for providing navigation services between interested locations. The increasing autonomy on the airborne drones in joint collaborative operations between different parties and their impact is analysed in [10].

Deciding the tasks to perform and the areas where to fly can be seen as a planning problem. In this work we are not dealing with the planning process performed by the swarm of drones. Therefore, we will not solve any optimality problems related to the decision process made by the swarms. For further details regarding the planning and optimality problem we refer the reader to [26, 28] where these problems are solved using techniques taken from artificial intelligence and automatic control [8]. Our aim is instead, to represent the various options and behavioural rules of the swarms with the use of a generic policy language.

An important challenge that arrises during the coordination and planning phases of drone systems, especially in collaborative scenarios, is the decision process of applicable actions for particular cases. A policy analysis for drone systems is developed in [19] that is able to capture and solve conflicting rules, and improve the efficiency of the used set of rules, based on argumentation and abductive reasoning [16], in particular it uses preference-based argumentation [5, 6, 24]. The work in [19] does not deal with the notion of swarm of drones and their operation. This analysis is an extension of the one proposed in [18, 21], that is used for enabling data sharing in different contexts by enforcing the correct data sharing agreements, and during forensics investigations for attributing cyber attacks to attackers [17]. Another interesting technique that uses an argumentation based analysis is introduced in [22], where the authors present a method for goal conflict resolution by analysing competing hypotheses and beliefs of stakeholders.

Section 2 presents a use case taken from a military scenario for a swarm of drones. Section 3 provides a definition and model of a swarm and describes as well how this swarm can operate. Section 4 provides example policies relevant to our scenario and how this set of policies controls the behaviour of the drones. Section 5 discusses the challenges and limitations in generating ad-hoc policies for the scenario and how new research can aid in solving these limitations. Finally we present the conclusions in Sect. 6.

2 Introduction to the Scenario: Collaborative Emergency Area Monitoring Between Military and Civil Organization

A military coalition has been formed to provide support to the government of a country that is suffering from severe flooding and whose resources (e.g., drones and aircraft) are occasionally attacked by rebels. There are two coalition partners (nations N_1 and N_2) and they each operate drones from their *forward operating bases* (FOBs). In addition *civil/humanitarian organisations* have allowed the coalition to command their drones that are operated from sites AM_1 and AM_2 as shown in Fig. 1.

The map shows the operating bases/sites, *emergency landing sites* (E_1, E_2, $\cdots$, E_5), and *no-fly-zones* that have been assigned to protect the health and safety of citizens living in clusters of towns in the south. The main flooding is in the west where there are a number of industrial plants that will cause pollution if the flood defences fail. Hence a set of surveillance *targets* (T_1, T_2, $\cdots$, T_7) has been established in order to monitor the water level of the rivers and lakes that are at risk of flooding, and the corresponding flood defences. Monitoring these

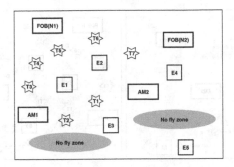

Fig. 1. Initial scenario representation

areas will allow appropriate action to be taken at the industrial plants, such as shutting them down, depending on the likelihood of flooding.

The commander handling the flooding emergency tasks a swarm of drones, formed from the coalition nations and civil/humanitarian organisations, to commence surveillance of the seven targets. The *lead drone* (D_1) is allocated three[1] further drones $(D_2, D_3$ and $D_4)$, and after planning assigns reconnaissance targets to the drones as shown in Fig. 2.

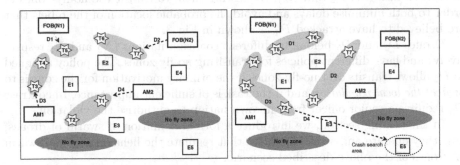

Fig. 2. Left: Reconnaissance targets assignation between the drones of a swarm. Right: Targets re-assignation after the emergency request made to D_4.

Some time later drone D_4 receives a weak *emergency* radio signal from a coalition manned aircraft saying that it has crashed and that the crew have survived but need assistance. The navigation equipment has failed and the location is described as "near E_5". D_4 authenticates the signal, reports it to the lead drone and decides autonomously to commence a search mission for the lost aircraft. The lead drone reassigns the surveillance roles and reports to the commander. The new state of the swarm is shown in Fig. 2.

---

[1] For the sake of simplicity, during the description of the scenario, we use a small number of drones.

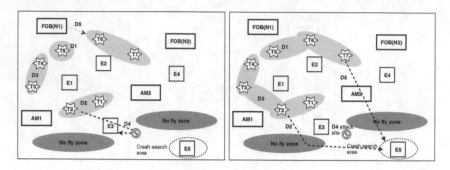

Fig. 3. Left: Target assignation update after the addition of D_5 into the swarm and D_4 emergency landing in E_3. Right: Replanning tasks assignation to respond the D_4's emergency.

Nation 1, (N_1), has a spare drone (D_5) and allocates it to the swarm, and the lead drone updates the plan. D_4 continues flying towards the search area, but comes under attack from suspected rebels and has to make an emergency landing, selecting site E_3, as shown in Fig. 3.

The lead drone replans the search activity in response to the emerging situation of D_4. Given the importance of the search and a risk assessment based on the health of the drones, the lead drone assigns the two nearest drones to the search task (i.e. D_2 and D_5), requesting them to transit the no-fly-zones in order to both minimise delays and avoid the probable location of the rebels that are believed to have attacked D_4 as shown in Fig. 3.

Drones D_2 and D_5 belong to different coalition nations (N_2 and N_1 respectively) and have different policies for transiting no-fly-zones. The policy assigned to D_2 allows transits over no-fly-zones if the primary motivation for the zone is to *protect the local population* and if the task is of sufficient importance. In contrast D_5 requires a senior officer from its own nation to authorise the violation.

In the coming section, we introduce a formal definition of swarm of drones, how they operate and a set of policies that regulate the behaviour of the swarm of drones of the above described scenario.

3   Definition and Operation of a Swarm

Despite growing literature about examples of swarming by drones, to the best of our knowledge there is not any fundamental work on the concept of swarming. In this section, we propose a definition and then discuss a model for swarming taking examples from the scenario in Sect. 2.

3.1   Definition of a Swarm of Drones

Let us first give a definition of a swarm.

Definition: *A swarm is a collection of assets that operate in a collaborative way to achieve a set of goals.*

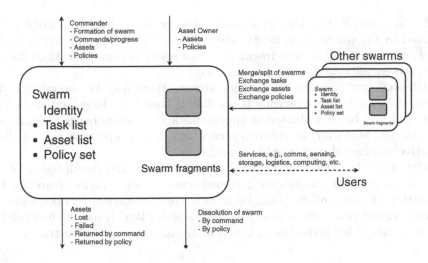

Fig. 4. The representation of the model of a swarm.

This definition does not constrain swarm membership to a homogenous set of drones. The swarm in our example scenario consists of military and civil/humanitarian drones so it is likely to be heterogeneous. Indeed, a swarm may be a mix of drones and land or maritime vehicles. We view a swarm primarily as a collaborative concept, and it may be composed of any assets that benefit from collaboration. Hence a swarm should be of the right size; too large and it becomes difficult to learn the appropriate individual behaviours to avoid unwanted and emergent behaviours. The assets are also a limited resource.

In our scenario the swarm had a *lead* drone that carried out the planning, although distributed control is an alternative approach. For example, the swarm members could work independently, reacting to the tasks the other members are performing to achieve the overall set of goals. The ASIMUT project [7] provides a further example of distributed control in a search mission where drones work collectively to cover the search space and the need to communicate is minimized by using predictable pseudo random paths. If a swarm has a leader there are varying levels of autonomy for the other members. At one extreme the leader could provide detailed requests to the member which would limit its automation (e.g., fly to a particular location, by using a certain route and at a specified speed and altitude). Alternatively, the requests can be at a much higher command level, allowing greater autonomy for the member to achieve its task (e.g., travel to and monitor this location).

As our scenario shows, a swarm is dynamic. It is *created* when required and achieves a set of goals that can be dynamic as well. A swarm *terminates* when the goals have been achieved, cancelled or become impractical. The *membership* of the swarm is dynamic; assets may be added, removed or fail, however, there will be finite number of assets that could be added to the swarm. Each asset has an owner, and as our scenario shows a swarm may have several asset owners.

The diagram in Fig. 4 shows a model of a swarm. It has an identity, tasks assigned by the commander, assets, and policies. The swarm will eventually be dissolved, and it may become fragmented as a result of communications limitations, a possibility considered in our scenario.

Although our scenario has a single swarm, there may be several swarms. Communication between swarms is possible if they have interoperable equipment, and may be on a planned or opportunistic basis to exchange tasks, assets and policies. Moreover, to ensure swarms have a near optimum size as their objectives change, they may split or merge.

The swarm in our scenario carried out surveillance and search tasks. Other tasks involving drones include environment sensing; crop spraying; searching for an emitter; provision of computing, storage or communications services; logistics delivery; decoy; protective convoy and acrobatic displays. It may be beneficial if a swarm undertakes several tasks concurrently, as our scenario illustrates.

3.2   Operating Swarms

In this section we introduce an example of how a policy enabled swarm could operate by exchanging messages between the entities. The messages have been designed for research purposes to show a step by step swarming sequence, and are not intended as an engineered solution. Moreover there are a number of simplifications made for brevity:

- Each swarm is controlled by a lead asset that is not lost, e.g. no provision is made for the appointment of a deputy leader with failover.
- Fully decentralised operation, without a lead asset, is not supported. However the assets can autonomously react to certain situations.
- All messages include an acknowledgement which is received successfully in the scenario under consideration.
- There is interoperability of command, policy and messaging between the civil/humanitarian and military drones. In practice, the communication between the different nations and civil/humanitarian drones is likely to be performed through the nation bases rather than directly from drone to drone.

In Fig. 5 we represent the message sequence diagram that corresponds to the scenario in Sect. 2. In detail, operation commences at time T_1 (times are shown to the left of the diagram) when the commander sends a *FormSwarm* message to appoint D_1 as the lead drone. Next, at time T_2, the drone owners allocate drones D_2, D_3 and D_4 to join the swarm using *JoinSwarm* messages. Note that the communications between the commander and the drone owners is not shown, it may for example have been verbal via military liaison officers.

The commander uses a *MissionCmd* message at time T_3 to task the swarm with surveillance. The lead drone plans the operation and in turn assigns roles to each drone using *MissionCmd* messages. The drones take off and fly to their surveillance areas (T_4), and commence surveillance when they arrive. Progress

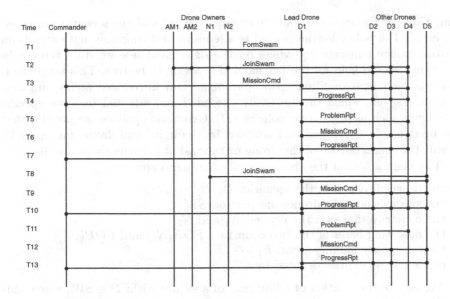

Fig. 5. The message sequence diagram of the scenario in Sect. 2.

is reported using a series of *ProgressRpt* messages (only the first message is illustrated). Surveillance reports will also be sent[2].

A manned coalition aircraft crashes near E_3 and the emergency signal is received by drone D_4 at time T_5. D_4 autonomously commences a search task and informs the lead drone using a *ProblemRpt* message. The lead drone replans the mission at time T_6, with the surveillance now carried out by drones D_1, D_2 and D_3, and the search carried out by D_4. Mission progress continues to be reported (T_7) and drone owner N_1 allocates drone D_5 to join the swarm at T_8. Once again the lead drone replans the mission, and sends the revised plans to all drones (T_9). On this occasion there is no change to the D_4 search plan. Mission progress continues to be reported (T_{10}).

Drone D_4 is attacked at time T_{11} and needs to make an emergency landing, selecting site E_3. This is reported to the lead drone using a *ProblemRpt* message. The lead drone replans the surveillance and search missions (T_{12}), with drones D_1 and D_3 carrying out modified surveillance roles and drones D_2 and D_5 commencing the search activity. Mission progress continues to be reported (T_{13}).

4   Policies to Support Autonomous Swarms

In this section, we introduce a policy representation of the rules that control the behaviour of the drones that are part of a swarm. In particular, we repre-

---

[2] For the sake of readability, we decided to do not illustrate the surveillance reports in the diagram.

sent, through the use of a policy language, the rules of the scenario presented in Sect. 2. The policy language used is a semi-natural language that extends an existing policy language [9], where on the right hand side we state the conditions that should hold for the left hand side action to be true. This language is based on an event-condition-action paradigm. Our introduced policy language is a generic one which can be easily extended and adapted to more specific paradigms such as generative policies [27]. Generative polices are policies that can be dynamically refined and adapted by the individual drone, for example, to suit the characteristic of the drone or the task it is currently performing.

The main actors of the above described scenario are:

- the drones involved in the scenario: $D_1, D_2, \cdots, D_5$;
- the swarm where the drones are part of: SW;
- the countries that own the drones: N_1 and N_2;
- the operating bases of the two countries: $FOB(N_1)$ and $FOB(N_2)$;
- the emergency landing areas: $E_1, \cdots, E_5$;
- other generic entities denoted by C.

We denote the relation of being part of a swarm with: $D \in SW$, where this predicate describes that drone D is part of swarm SW. The property of being the *lead drone* in a swarm is denoted by $Leader(SW)$, where $D = Leader(SW)$ represents that drone D is the leader of swarm SW. As described in the previously, we expect to have just one lead drone for a swarm. Being the leader implies being part of the swarm as well, $D = Leader(SW) \rightarrow D \in SW$. For the sake of simplicity, we denote the lead drone by L instead of D. In case a given entity C is not part of the swarm, then this entity cannot be its leader: $C \notin SW \rightarrow C \neq Leader(SW)$. We denote by $req(Sub, Tar, Act, T)$ the predicate that represents sending a request at the instant of time T from the subject Sub to the target Tar for performing a certain action Act. The predicate $perform(Sub, Act, T, permit)$ describes that subject Sub is permitted to start carrying out the action Act, and this permission is given at the instant of time T. Once the perform predicate is permitted then Sub will start performing the granted action:

$$do(Sub, Act, T) \leftarrow perform(Sub, Act, T, permit). \tag{1}$$

For the sake of simplicity, we omit this predicate in the future and every time a perform predicate is permitted we understand that the action will start to be executed on the same instant of time. In the scenario a drone/swarm is requested to perform a certain $Task$ that can be accepted or denied. Therefore, the perform predicate will be of the form: $perform(Sub, Task, T, permit/deny)$.

Given the drones that are part of a swarm, they are permitted to start carrying out actions that are given/requested just from their lead drone. The drones do not perform the tasks requested from other drones that are not the nominated swarm leader[3]. These rules are represented as below:

---

[3] We assume that we deal with one request for performing an action at a time, and in the case the leader requests an action to a drone while it is still performing a previous one, then it drops the previous action and starts the new one.

$$perform(D, Task, T, permit) \leftarrow D \in SW, \ L \in SW, \ L = Leader(SW),$$
$$req(L, D, Task, T). \tag{2}$$

$$perform(D, Task, T, deny) \leftarrow D \in SW, L \neq Leader(SW),$$
$$req(L, D, Task, T). \tag{3}$$

In the case there is an *emergency* where humans of a coalition are involved and the drones receive a request to perform a certain task from them, then the drones accept the requested action, as described in the following rule.

$$perform(D, Task, T, permit) \leftarrow Emerg(C), \ req(C, D, Task, T), \ D \in SW,$$
$$C \neq Leader(SW), \ C \in Coalition(D),$$
$$Human(C). \tag{4}$$

In the above rule, given an entity denoted by C, that makes a request to a certain drone D to perform a task, where this entity is in an emergency situation $Emerg(C)$, it is a human $Human(C)$, in a coalition relation with D, denoted by $Coalition(D)$, and is not part of the swarm where D is part of, therefore not the swarm leader, then the drone is permitted to start performing the requested task. This permission is given as the request came from a human that is a coalition member and is in an emergency. Note that we define the set of all entities that are in coalition with a given subject S by $Coalition(S)$. Thus, we use the relation $\in$ for denoting when a certain object O is in coalition with S, e.g., $O \in Coalition(S)$, means that object O is part of the same coalition as S.

When the drone accepts an action from an entity that is not its leader, then it sends a notification ($Emerg\_N$) to its leader as well[4].

$$send(D, L, Emerg\_N, T, permit) \leftarrow L = Leader(SW), D \in SW,$$
$$C \neq Leader(SW), req(C, D, Task, T),$$
$$perform(D, Task, T, permit). \tag{5}$$

The task given to the drone is composed of the reconnaissance targets that are translated into the areas where the drone should fly to reach the targets. The predicate $PermArea(Task, Coalition(D))$ holds when all the areas to be passed by drone D, to perform the task $Task$, are permitted flying areas for the coalition where drone D is part of, $Coalition(D)$, and there is not any no-fly-zone. In the case in the given $Task$ there are not any no-fly-zone, then the drone is permitted to fly and perform the task.

$$fly(D, Task, T, permit) \leftarrow perform(D, Task, T, permit),$$
$$PermArea(Task, Coalition(D)). \tag{6}$$

In the case there is at least one no-fly-zone area included in the requested task, then the drone is not permitted to fly for performing that task.

$$fly(D, Task, T, deny) \leftarrow perform(D, Task, T, permit),$$
$$\textbf{not } PermArea(Task, Coalition(D)). \tag{7}$$

---

[4] To be precise, rules (5)–(10) would not have $perform(D, Task, T, permit)$, but $do(D, Task, T)$. As explained previously, we decided for the sake of understandability to omit the *do* predicate, and use this short-hand annotation.

In the case the drones need to fly into no-fly-zones, then there are different rules for permitting it, and they vary from the drones' owner. The drones of nation N_2 can fly into no-fly-zones in case there is an emergency involving humans.

$$fly(D, Task, T, permit) \leftarrow D \in SW, D \in N_2, Emerg(C), C \in Coalition(D),$$
$$Human(C), perform(D, Task, T, permit),$$
$$\textbf{not } PermArea(Task, SW).$$
$$(8)$$

The rule is different for drones of country N_1. For permitting drones of N_1 to fly into no-fly-zones, an authorization request, $auth\_req$ to the FOB of N_1 for $Task$ needs to be generated. In the case N_1 accepts this request, then an authorization is issued for the drone to fly into the non permitted area.

$$auth\_req(FOB(N_1), D, Task, T) \leftarrow D \in SW, D \in N_1,$$
$$perform(D, Task, T, permit), \quad (9)$$
$$\textbf{not } PermArea(Task, SW).$$

$$fly(D, Task, T, permit) \leftarrow perform(D, Task, T, permit), D \in SW, D \in N_1,$$
$$\textbf{not } Perm\_Area(Task, SW),$$
$$Auth(FOB(N_1), D, Task, permit).$$
$$(10)$$

Rule (7) is in conflict with rule (8) and (10). In our scenario rules (8) and (10) prevails over rule (7), as they are more specific. For solving the conflicts between policies we can use an abductive and argumentation reasoning for conflict resolution as in [18, 21].

If the drone finds itself in an emergency situation, then it is permitted to land in a designated emergency area allocated to its swarm. In this case, the drone notifies its leader with an emergency landing notification.

$$land(D, E, T, permit) \leftarrow Emerg(D), D \in SW, E \in Emerg\_Area(SW). \quad (11)$$

$$send(D, L, EL\_N, T, permit) \leftarrow Emerg(D), D \in SW, L = Leader(SW). \quad (12)$$

In the above case, E is one of the emergency areas of the given swarm ($Emerg\_Area(SW)$), and the notification sent to the leader of the swarm is denoted by EL_N.

5   Scenario and Policy Discussion

In this section we consider some variants of the scenario described in Sect. 2 to highlight the challenges in generating and using policies for autonomous swarms.

5.1   Communications Between Drones

The first discussion is around communications between drones. Drone D_4 was the first asset to receive the emergency signal from the crashed aircraft and on the basis of this authenticated signal D_4 decided autonomously to commence a search operation, and also reported the situation to the lead drone. This report was critical because D_4 subsequently came under attack; what if D_4 had been unable communicate with the lead drone due to the contested communications, and the subsequent attack had damaged the drone and it had failed to reach the emergency landing site?

If D_4 was the only asset to receive the emergency signal, and D_4 was damaged before it had communicated the news, then the mission would be delayed until the emergency was detected in other ways, e.g., a timeout on arrival or after failing to submit or respond to agreed communications. This may increase the risk to the survivors of the crash. If on the other hand, D_4 knew/suspected that it was the only asset to receive the emergency signal then policies could be used to guide the drone to position itself to increase the probability of communicating with the coalition. This decision is a trade off between delaying the search and the risk that the knowledge of the crash is lost.

This example highlights the possible conflicts between policies such as rules (8) and (10) with (7), in Sect. 4, and clearly in any policy system a strategy for dealing with conflicts is required. A proposed solution would be to use the argumentation and abductive reasoning procedure introduced in [18,21], and more specifically for drones [19], where the rules are left as they are, and priorities between them are introduced. The priority relation between rules is denoted by $\prec$, where $r_1 \prec r_2$ means that rule r_2 takes priority over rule r_1. In our scenario, we have that rule (8) prevails over rule (7), and rule (10) prevails over rule (7), denoted correspondingly by (7) $\prec$ (8) and (7) $\prec$ (10).

5.2 Policy Sharing

The second discussion point is around sharing of policies. In the scenario we have drones from civil/humanitarian organisations and from military organizations of two nations that have different policies for transiting the no-fly-zones. The lead drone (D_1) is part of nation N_1, so therefore should have access to the policies for other drones that are part of the same nation, such as D_5, who it instructs to transit a no-fly-zone in order to respond to the crashed aircraft. However, the lead drone (D_1) also instructs D_2 from N_2 to respond and transit the no-fly-zone. If the polices are shared between the two nations, then the lead drone can successfully plan the tasks. However sharing policies with another nation could present a security risk.

In our scenario we are working with two types of drones, military and civil/humanitarian organizations. The rules for sharing information and data can be different for both of them, e.g., more restrictive from the military drones side. For future work in managing the different behavioural rules between the two types of drones we suggest to use the policy analysis introduced in [19]. In the case there is a need of performing data alteration, or restriction of data quality when information is shared between drones that have different owners and different relations between each other, we propose to use the data alteration mechanism introduced in [20]. The proposed alteration mechanism is based on the same policy language we extend in this work, and is attached to the data in a similar mechanism as the sticky policies.

One of the limitations with existing policy based architectures is a lack of flexibility and customisation of the polices at the individual drone. This limits the automation of the drone to adapt the polices to its own characteristics or to a changing environment. A generative policy architecture [27] aims to solve this by allowing an initial policy specification called a generative policy to be distributed to all drones, but allowing it to be adapted at the individual drone, a simple example for drone systems is discussed in [10].

6   Conclusions

In this paper we have defined a realistic scenario that can be used to investigate and trial autonomous swarms of drones. In summary a military coalition of drones from two nations and humanitarian/civil organisations work together to monitor areas prone to natural disasters, such as flooding. In this area vehicles are suspect to occasional attacks from rebels, and while monitoring an area of interest a drone receives a distress signal from a coalition aircraft that it needs to investigate and then itself comes under attack. Throughout this the drones need to work together and react to the changing situation in order to complete their existing monitoring tasks and the additional high priority search and rescue incidents.

We have defined a swarm as a *collection of assets that operate in a collaborative way to achieve a set of goals* and provided a model for swarm. The model identifies that a swarm has an identity, task list, asset list and a policy set. It also allows assets to join or leave the swarm, and interacts with assess owners, commanders and other swarms. An example of how a policy enabled swarm can operate has been provided, assuming that it is controlled by a leader.

A set of polices have been defined to control the behaviour of the drones. These policies cover areas such as whether the drones can accept the given task and if they can transit no-fly-zones. We have introduced a policy language using a semi natural language approach based on the event-condition paradigm. This language can easily be extended and adapted to more specific paradigms.

We have then discussed the challenges the scenario introduces and the limitations of existing policy based solutions. We then pull together some interesting future work that can be done by using generative polices and approaches for communications between coalitions that can improve and perhaps solve these limitations.

Acknowledgments. This research was sponsored by the U.S. Army Research Laboratory and the U.K. Ministry of Defence under Agreement Number W911NF-16-3-0001. The views and conclusions contained in this document are those of the authors and should not be interpreted as representing the official policies, either expressed or implied, of the U.S. Army Research Laboratory, the U.S. Government, the U.K. Ministry of Defence or the U.K. Government. The U.S. and U.K. Governments are autho-

References

1. Darpa: Service academies swarm challenge live-fly competition (2017). https://www.youtube.com/watch?v=RZ-CKA4fUhg

2. Amazon.com Inc.: Amazon Prime Air. https://www.amazon.com/b?node=8037720011

3. Amazon.com Inc.: Determining safe access with a best-equipped, best-served model for small unmanned aircraft systems (2015). https://images-na.ssl-images-amazon.com/images/G/01/112715/download/Amazon_Determining_Safe_Access_with_a_Best-Equipped_Best-Served_Model_for_sUAS.pdf

4. Amazon.com Inc.: Revising the airspace model for the safe integration of small unmanned aircraft systems' (2015). https://images-na.ssl-images-amazon.com/images/G/01/112715/download/Amazon_Revising_the_Airspace_Model_for_the_Safe_Integration_of_sUAS.pdf

5. Amgoud, L., Dimopoulos, Y., Moraitis, P.: Making decisions through preference-based argumentation. In: Brewka, G., Lang, J. (eds.) KR, pp. 113–123. AAAI Press (2008)

6. Bondarenko, A., Dung, P.M., Kowalski, R.A., Toni, F.: An abstract, argumentation-theoretic approach to default reasoning. Artif. Intelli. **93**(1–2), 63–101 (1997)

7. Bouvry, P., et al.: ASIMUT project: aid to SItuation management based on MUltimodal, MUltiUAVs, MUltilevel acquisition techniques. In: Proceedings of the 3rd Workshop on Micro Aerial Vehicle Networks, Systems, and Applications, pp. 17–20. ACM (2017)

8. Cortes, J., Martinez, S., Karatas, T., Bullo, F.: Coverage control for mobile sensing networks. In: IEEE International Conference on Robotics and Automation (ICRA 2002), vol. 2, pp. 1327–1332. IEEE (2002)

9. Craven, R., Lobo, J., Ma, J., Russo, A., Lupu, E.C., Bandara, A.K.: Expressive policy analysis with enhanced system dynamicity. In: Proceedings of the 2009 ACM Symposium on Information, Computer and Communications Security, ASIACCS, pp. 239–250 (2009)

10. Cullen, A., Williams, B., Bertino, E., Arunkumar, S., Karafili, E., Lupu, E.: Mission support for drones: a policy based approach. In: Proceedings of the 3rd Workshop on Micro Aerial Vehicle Networks, Systems, and Applications, DroNet@MobiSys 2017, pp. 7–12 (2017)

11. (EASA): EASA concept of operation for drones: a risk based approach to regulation of unmanned aircraft (2015). https://www.easa.europa.eu/sites/default/files/dfu/204696_EASA_concept_drone_brochure_web.pdf (2015)

12. Gharibi, M., Boutaba, R., Waslander, S.L.: Internet of drones. IEEE Access **4**, 1148–1162 (2016)

13. Hunjet, R., Stevens, T., Elliot, M., Fraser, B., George, P.: Survivable communications and autonomous delivery service a generic swarming framework enabling communications in contested environments. In: IEEE Military Communications Conference (MILCOM), pp. 788–793 (2017)

14. Google Inc.: Google UAS Airspace System Overview (2015). https://utm.arc.nasa.gov/docs/GoogleUASAirspaceSystemOverview5pager[1].pdf

15. Joint doctrine note 2/11: the UK approach to unmanned aircraft systems, March 2011
16. Kakas, A.C., Kowalski, R.A., Toni, F.: Abductive logic programming. J. log. Comput. **2**(6), 719–770 (1992)
17. Karafili, E., Kakas, A.C., Spanoudakis, N.I., Lupu, E.C.: Argumentation-based security for social good. In: AAAI Fall Symposium Series, pp. 164–170 (2017)
18. Karafili, E., Lupu, E.C.: Enabling data sharing in contextual environments: policy representation and analysis. In: Proceedings of the 22nd ACM on Symposium on Access Control Models and Technologies, SACMAT, pp. 231–238 (2017)
19. Karafili, E., Lupu, E.C., Arunkumar, S., Bertino, E.: Argumentation-based policy analysis for drone systems. In: 2017 IEEE Smart-World/SCALCOM/UIC/ATC/CBDCom/IOP/SCI, pp. 1–6 (2017)
20. Karafili, E., Lupu, E.C., Cullen, A., Williams, B., Arunkumar, S., Calo, S.B.: Improving data sharing in data rich environments. In: IEEE International Conference on Big Data, BigData 2017, pp. 2998–3005 (2017)
21. Karafili, E., Spanaki, K., Lupu, E.C.: An argumentation reasoning approach for data processing. Comput. Ind. **94**, 52–61 (2018)
22. Murukannaiah, P.K., Kalia, A.K., Telangy, P.R., Singh, M.P.: Resolving goal conflicts via argumentation-based analysis of competing hypotheses. In: IEEE 23rd International Requirements Engineering Conference (RE), pp. 156–165 (2015)
23. NASA: NASA UTM 2015: the next era of aviation (2015). https://utm.arc.nasa.gov/utm2015.shtml
24. Prakken, H., Sartor, G.: Argument-based extended logic programming with defeasible priorities. J. Appl. Non-Class. Log. **7**(1), 25–75 (1997)
25. Reynolds, C.W.: Flocks, herds and schools: a distributed behavioral model. In: ACM SIGGRAPH Computer Graphics, vol. 21, pp. 25–34. ACM (1987)
26. Steve, O.E., Hanks, D.W., Draper, D.: An approach to planning with incomplete information. In: Third International Conference Principles of Knowledge Representation and Reasoning (KR 1992), p. 115 (1992)
27. Verma, D.C., et al.: Generative policy model for autonomic management. In: 2017 IEEE SmartWorld/SCALCOM/UIC/ATC/CBDCom/IOP/SCI, pp. 1–6 (2017)
28. Weld, D.S.: Recent advances in ai planning. AI Mag. **20**(2), 93 (1999)
29. Google X: Project Wing. https://x.company/wing/

Violation Detection and Countermeasures

A Logic-Based Reasoner for Discovering Authentication Vulnerabilities Between Interconnected Accounts

Erisa Karafili[1]([✉]), Daniele Sgandurra[2], and Emil Lupu[1]

[1] Department of Computing, Imperial College London, London, England
{e.karafili,e.c.lupu}@imperial.ac.uk
[2] Information Security Group, Royal Holloway, University of London,
Egham, England
daniele.sgandurra@rhul.ac.uk

Abstract. With users being more reliant on online services for their daily activities, there is an increasing risk for them to be threatened by cyber-attacks harvesting their personal information or banking details. These attacks are often facilitated by the strong interconnectivity that exists between online accounts, in particular due to the presence of shared (e.g., replicated) pieces of user information across different accounts. In addition, a significant proportion of users employs pieces of information, e.g. used to recover access to an account, that are easily obtainable from their social networks accounts, and hence are vulnerable to correlation attacks, where a malicious attacker is either able to perform password reset attacks or take full control of user accounts.

This paper proposes the use of verification techniques to analyse the possible vulnerabilities that arises from shared pieces of information among interconnected online accounts. Our primary contributions include a logic-based reasoner that is able to discover vulnerable online accounts, and a corresponding tool that provides modelling of user accounts, their interconnections, and vulnerabilities. Finally, the tool allows users to perform security checks of their online accounts and suggests possible countermeasures to reduce the risk of compromise.

Keywords: Logic-based reasoner · Logic analyzer · Authentication
Interconnected accounts

1 Introduction

With reliance on Information Technology (IT) growing, more and more services are being gradually digitised, and users are getting accustomed to use online accounts to handle almost all their digital life, from banking accounts to day-to-day communications – the so called "digital footprint" [6,10]. Typically, when registering for an online account, besides creating his/her credentials, a user is required to enter an email address for verification as well as providing answers to

© Springer Nature Switzerland AG 2018
A. Saracino and P. Mori (Eds.): ETAA 2018, LNCS 11263, pp. 73–87, 2018.
https://doi.org/10.1007/978-3-030-04372-8_7

a set of predefined questions as a way for password recovery (also called *cognitive passwords*). Depending on the nature of the online account created, users may also be asked to provide other pieces of information, such as a billing address, birthday, name of their pet and so on. However, different accounts end up being logically connected by virtue of having the same owner, e.g. because they share a common password, or because some pieces of information (e.g., date of birth) are shared across these accounts. This allows attackers to perform attacks such as *credential stuffing* cyber-attacks[1], where stolen account credentials (i.e., username/email address and passwords) are used to gain unauthorized access to user accounts on online services through large-scale automated login requests (e.g., using tools such as Sentry MBA [3]) on critical websites (e.g., to perform e-banking activities). The danger in this type of attacks comes from the fact that many users reuse credentials across many different websites and, therefore, the compromise of one account, typically on non-critical websites having few resources and/or motivations to protect those credentials, can have widespread repercussions to other accounts as well. Therefore, the automated analysis of security flaws within interconnected accounts is an important issue.

Another example that shows how interconnections between online accounts pose security threats to users are recovery security questions. Consider a user having an online account with a recovery security question "What is your date of birth?". However, empirical studies have found out that a significant proportion of users have security information which are easily attainable on social networks, and hence are vulnerable to reset attacks [20]. A real life example would be that of Mr. Mat Honan, who came under media scrutiny when his online accounts were hacked progressively, starting from his iCloud account. In fact, attackers obtained the last four digits of his credit card number through Amazon [18]. Then, the attackers were able to fool the Apple technical support staff into giving them a temporary password to Honan's iCloud account as they assumed his identity by providing the partial credit card number. From there, the attackers continued to gain access to Honan's Gmail and Twitter accounts using the iCloud account previously compromised. Furthermore, since iCloud Keychain keeps and remembers passwords for online and offline accounts across authorised devices, attackers were in turn able to gain access to all accounts linked to this service. This incident shows how conflicting security policies of different online services can be a disadvantage for users, and it also highlights the chain reactions among accounts that can occur after a single account is compromised.

Even if it is simple to devise measures to prevent attacks for a small number of accounts (e.g., avoiding the use of the same password across different account), however, an analysis of data from more than 20,000 users in 2015 found that the average user has 90 online accounts [4], and so even simple policies are difficult to be enforced in such large contexts. In addition, this analysis found that in the U.S. there is an average of 130 accounts assigned to a single email address. Hence, there are too many pieces of information to be remembered, and too many interconnections among accounts that are potential vulnerabilities. As

---

[1] https://www.owasp.org/index.php/Credential_stuffing.

such, there can be multiple ways of exploit for the attacker, and it is impractical and inefficient for a user to go through all of his/her accounts to find flaws. Therefore, there is a need for an automatic reasoner that is able to analyse all the accounts and their interconnections looking for known vulnerabilities or potential ones.

This paper introduces a logic-based approach to identify security flaws in interconnected user accounts. To this end, we propose a reasoner to model accounts, identify threats and propose countermeasures. The proposed reasoner supports different types of online accounts and enables users to find compromised accounts as well as corresponding countermeasures to protect these accounts. We have developed a prototype tool that, given as input the user's accounts information, returns the compromised accounts and proposes countermeasures. In addition, further vulnerabilities or connections between accounts can be added to perform a 'what-if' analysis. Then, given the interconnected accounts and their related vulnerabilities, the tool shows the steps of the possible exploitation of an account. Finally, the tool focuses on the accounts where the exploits are simpler and easier to achieve, and provides a set of countermeasures to reduce the risk of account exploitation.

The main contributions of this paper are:

- We formalize the problem of vulnerabilities that derive from interconnected devices.
- We propose a reasoner to model user accounts and vulnerabilities, and the interconnections among different accounts.
- We implement a tool that, given the user accounts, finds the relations between accounts and shows the dependences between interconnected accounts that can be exploited by malicious users.

The rest of the paper is structured as follows. In Sect. 2 we describe related works. Then, in Sect. 3, we describe the proposed framework, which is used (i) to formally represent online accounts, (ii) to model existing vulnerabilities in interconnected accounts, (iii) to simulate interactions across accounts, (iv) to analyse security flaws, and (v) to generate corresponding countermeasures. In Sect. 4 we describe the implementation of the reasoner, while in Sect. 5 we report some preliminary evaluations of our framework. Finally, in Sect. 6 we conclude the paper.

2   Related Work

Model checking is a viable way to analyse security flaw in interconnected accounts as it supports partial verification [2]. There is no need to provide a complete specification and, hence, more focus can be put on essential properties which need to be fulfilled. Besides, when a property is invalidated, diagnostic information is provided through the trace and this is particularly useful when determining countermeasures for these vulnerabilities. There are, however, certain disadvantages to using model checking as a technique for verification. In particular, model checking suffers from the state space explosion problem and, if the number of states required is very large to be efficiently represented on the computer memory, then the computation may take a long time [21]. MulVAL is a logic-based framework which models the interaction of software bugs with system and network configurations [17] and analyse security vulnerabilities of the network. MulVAL is implemented first by capturing the database of known vulnerabilities, then scanning the system for configuration information and also at the same time matching the known vulnerabilities to the system. These pieces of information are then encoded using Datalog, a subset of the Prolog language. MulVAL captures system interactions using a set of pre-defined rules, and analysis on the security level of the system is carried out once this preparation is done.

Attack graphs (AGs) have long been used as an effective way of assessing security threats in a network system. AGs provide a visual representations of how an exploit, or a series of exploits, can affect different hosts in a network in terms of node compromise. In the literature, there are mainly two types of attack graphs: the first one, state-based AGs, shows how an attack happens, while the second one, logical AGs, shows why an attack happens. State-based AGs [9,24] result in directed graphs, where each node represents the state of the whole network after a successful atomic attack. However, state-based AGs also suffer from state explosion issues, and empirical data has shown that graph generation procedure takes a much longer time compared to the model checking phase [23]. Moreover, these graphs contain duplicate attack paths that differ only in the order of the attack steps, which also increase the complexity of the graph, limiting the applicability of state-based representations to very small networks [8,16]. Therefore, state-based AGs do not scale well for a large number of accounts. The scalability problems of state-based representations are overcome with *logical AGs*, which are bipartite graphs that represent dependencies between exploits and security conditions [1,8]. These representations rely on the monotonicity principle: this principle states that an attacker never relinquishes privileges once obtained. Nevertheless, a suitable method to model the system needs to be chosen before generating the attack graph. The uncertainty about the attacker's behaviour makes Bayesian networks more suitable to model AG as well as to perform static and dynamic security risk assessment. For this reason, several techniques have also been proposed in the literature for performing inference on Bayesian attack graphs (BAGs). For example, forward-backward propagation is proposed in [19] to compute the unconditional probabilities. More recently, the JT algorithm was proposed in [13] for exact inference in BAGs to efficiently compute the exact unconditional probabilities by using a probabilistic message passing scheme. However, the applicability of JT to large networks is limited, especially when the AGs are dense. Therefore, the work in [14] shows how approximate inference techniques can be applied to attack graphs, so that the analysis scales linearly in the number of nodes for both static and dynamic analysis, making such analyses viable for larger networks.

3 A Logic-Based Reasoner to Model Online Accounts

In this section, we describe how the proposed reasoner models online accounts, simulates interactions across accounts, analyzes security flaws, and generates corresponding countermeasures.

3.1 Modelling of Online Accounts

Our logic-based reasoner represents the various accounts by firstly uniquely identifying them through their service provider and username, and then by associating them with other pieces of information regarding the user, e.g. password. In addition, the reasoner considers the user information associated to an account as either private or public, and allows users to select the type of authentication procedure used for every account, e.g. using a single sign-on or using the specific service provider. Another important entity modelled by our framework is the user, which is represented through the following attributes: name, gender, date of birth, mobile number, city, home-town, location, workplace, job and address (other fields can be easily added). To analyse possible vulnerabilities, every account is associated with an access policy which states who should be able to access the account. Anyone outside of this group of people/entities, who are allowed access to the account, should not be able to access the account, or it will be considered a violation of this policy. In case an entity/user, which is not part of the entities/users that are allowed to access the account, accesses the account, then this is considered a violation of the policy, and this is modelled in our reasoner as:

$$policyViolation(Account, Access) \leftarrow hasAccessed(Account, Access),$$
$$\textbf{not } allowAccess(Account, Access).$$

where the left side of "←" represents the conclusion of the engine policy (also called *rules*), while the right side represents the preconditions that should be satisfied for the rule to be triggered and the conclusion to be satisfied. For the sake of simplicity and presentation purpose, in our rules' representations we do not use the AND logical connector ("∧"), but we substitute it simply with "," – we still use the OR logical connector and represent it with "∨".

Finally, the reasoner is also used to represent generic attackers that carries out exploits by using stolen/retrieved/inferred account's information. In the reasoner, there are three main categories of exploits that an attacker can use to compromise an account:

- the attacker is able to find the credentials of the account;
- the account uses single sing-on verification and the attacker is able to exploit it;
- the attacker knows the username and is able to reset the password of the account.

3.2 Vulnerabilities of Accounts

We now describe the list of vulnerabilities that we have modelled in our reasoner. We consider vulnerabilities for individual accounts, as well as vulnerabilities that arise when linking different accounts. In the following, we describe these vulnerabilities together with their representation in our reasoner.

Vulnerabilities for Individual Accounts. The vulnerabilities for individual accounts are vulnerabilities independent from the connection between accounts, and these are:

- Publicly-available username: namely, when the chosen username can be obtained easily. This might happen in some online forums where the used nicknames or avatars replicates the username. This vulnerability is modelled as:

$$vulExists(publicUsername, X) \leftarrow account(X), username(X, U), public(U).$$

- Publicly-available email: usually service providers request an email address from the user, often used for password recovery. When a user forgets his/her password, a reset link is sent to this address to allow the user to change/reset the password. As a result, having this piece of information available means that the attacker can use some of his/her efforts in exploiting this email account as well. This vulnerability is modelled as:

$$vulExists(publicEmail, X) \leftarrow account(X), email(X, E), public(E).$$

- Commonly-used password: a list of commonly used passwords are published every year by several institutions [5]. If the user selects such a password, the attacker does not even need to carry out a dictionary attack to obtain the password of the particular account. This vulnerability is modelled as:

$$vulExists(commonPW, X) \leftarrow account(X), pwAccount(X, pw),$$
$$commonPW(pw).$$

- Password contains name of user: it is not uncommon to find users using just their name as passwords. This vulnerability is modelled as:

$$vulExists(sameName\&PW, X) \leftarrow account(X), nameofUser(X, N),$$
$$pwAccount(X, pw),$$
$$(N = pw \vee similar(N, pw)).$$

We use the $similar(N, Pw)$ predicate as the password can be a simple variation of the name, thus, they are not exactly the same but similar[2].

---

[2] The predicate $similar(A, B)$ states that A and B are very similar to each other and by knowing A the attacker can infer easily B, and vice versa.

– Password contains username of user: even if some website disallows the use of the username as password, not every website enforces this rule. This vulnerability is modelled as:

$$vulExists(sameUsername\&PW, X) \leftarrow account(X), username(X, U),$$
$$pwAccount(X, pw),$$
$$(U = pw \lor similar(U, pw)).$$

– Password is weak: while several websites provide a password robustness check, users are able to find (sometime ingenious) alternative ways to bypass these checks and provide a weak password. This vulnerability is modelled as:

$$vulExists(weakPW, X) \leftarrow account(X), pwAccount(X, pw), weakPW(pw).$$

– Password unchanged for too long: a password which has not been changed for long, if weak, can be easily found due to dictionary attacks. This vulnerability is modelled as:

$$vulExists(oldPW, X) \leftarrow account(X), pwAccount(X, pw), oldPW(pw).$$

Vulnerabilities due to Account Connections. In the following we describe those vulnerabilities that involve linkage across different accounts that are owned by the same user/entity, which are:

– Repeated passwords: many users use the same passwords across different accounts. This means that if an attacker knows (or is able to retrieve) the password to an account, he/she also can access all the accounts which reuses this particular password. This vulnerability is modelled as:

$$vulExists(repeatPW, X, Y) \leftarrow account(X), account(Y), X \neq Y,$$
$$pwAccount(X, pw_1), pwAccount(Y, pw_2),$$
$$pw_1 = pw_2.$$

– Repeated usernames: suppose an attacker knows the username of a specific account, the attacker can attempt to log in a different online account with the same username to check if the account exists. This vulnerability is modelled as:

$$vulExists(repeatUsername, X, Y) \leftarrow account(X), account(Y), X \neq Y,$$
$$username(X, U_1), username(Y, U_2),$$
$$U_1 = U_2.$$

– Information required for password reset available (publicly or through the use of another account). There are mainly two methods used for password reset: the first method entails sending a recovery link to the associated email address, while the second one requires the user to answer a set of security questions. In this last case, the information required for answering security questions may be available publicly or in another account that the attacker already has access to. This means that the attacker can use this piece of information to compromise the account of the user by resetting the passwords. This vulnerability is modelled as:

$$vulExists(publicRecoveryInfo, X) \leftarrow account(X), recovery(X, Info),$$
$$public(Info).$$

$$vulExists(recoveryInfoInAcc, X, Y) \leftarrow account(X), recovery(X, Info),$$
$$account(Y), X \neq Y,$$
$$inAccount(Y, Info).$$

In Fig. 1 we show a graphical representation of the dependencies between accounts and possible vulnerabilities that might allow attackers to get access to a particular account, which we have modelled in our reasoner.

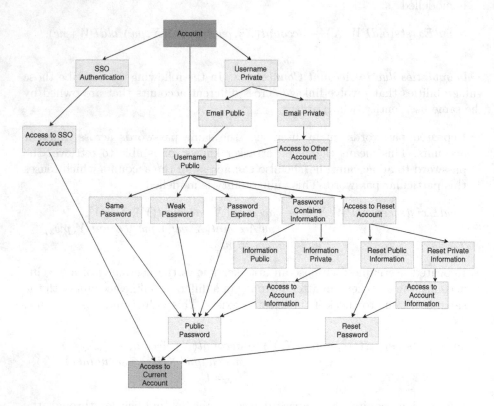

Fig. 1. Attack tree of an account based on the attackers' knowledge

3.3   Metrics for Account Compromise Analysis

Let us now give a brief overview of the metrics we have introduced in our reasoner to provide a measure of the extent of compromised accounts. The first two metrics are non-path analysis metrics while the remaining ones are metrics related to the paths that attackers can follow to access the account.

- An interesting metric to use is the *network compromise percentage* (NCP) [12], which measures the proportion of the network that was compromised/attacked successfully by the attacker. In our reasoner, this metrics represents the proportion of accounts that are compromised by the attacker. The reasoner allocates a higher weight to accounts that hold sensitive information, e.g. bank or card details, or to accounts that have information about other accounts.
- To analyse the generated graphs the reasoner uses the *weakest adversary* metric, which measures the security of the weakest component in the network [7]. Using this metric, the reasoner assumes that the set of accounts are as secure as their weakest component.
- The first path metric the reasoner checks is the *shortest path* [15], which represents the smallest number of steps leading to the attack goal. Knowing the shortest path helps the reasoner in developing a countermeasure, as we expect the attackers to choose the most efficient way to reach their target. Please note that the shortest path is not necessarily the easiest path. Therefore, this metric does not always provide a consistent evaluation of the attacks.
- Another metrics in the reasoner is the *number of paths*, which represents the number of different attacks/exploits that can be carried out to compromise the same account [15]. This metrics can also be used to define the account with the highest risk of being compromised, as the higher the number of exploits, the higher the number of vulnerabilities that can be used by the attacker. Having a higher number of vulnerabilities does not necessarily mean that the vulnerabilities have higher chances on being exploited as no information is provided on their difficulties on being exploited.
- The *mean path length* [11] is the arithmetic average of all the paths lengths that, starting from an initial state, bring to the goal account. This metric is relevant in determining the average level of effort required to compromise an account [9]. Its drawback is that the value might be the same even when there is an increase in the number of paths.
- To evaluate which are the outliers when it comes to different exploits, the reasoner uses the *standard deviation of path lengths*. This metrics is useful when generating countermeasures, as we want to focus on specific attack paths that are more likely to be exploited.
- The reasoner also uses the *mode* and *median* of path lengths as they are less likely to be influenced from outliers values. The *normalised mean path length* gives a better security estimate as it is based on both the number of paths as well as the path lengths, hence addressing the key criticism of the mean path length metric. The reasoner aggregates the functions of both the mean path length and the total number of paths.

The different metrics pertain to different types of conclusions a user can draw from the generated graph. In more detail, the number of paths, shortest path and mean path length metrics quantify the overall security level of the network or an individual account. Therefore, these metrics can be used as a basis of comparison before and after a countermeasure is implemented to find out the effectiveness of such a countermeasure. Instead, the mean path for an individual account and the standard deviation can be employed together to find which account requires the greatest attention. For instance, suppose the user wishes only to secure the most vulnerable accounts, the reasoner can present countermeasures only pertaining to accounts with mean path length below the network mean or below a certain percentage.

In the following we first describe the threat model used in the reasoner, and how the reasoner selects the countermeasures.

3.4   Threat Model and Countermeasure Analysis

In the threat model, we make the assumption that every attacker has all the possible pieces of information that it can obtain, which is not necessarily true as sometimes the attacker cannot find connections between accounts or cannot identify the public information needed for compromising an account. Similarly, we assume that an attacker knows a piece of information in case it is public, or if the information is stored in an account where the attacker has access to. In addition, we assume that an attacker can compromise an account if s/he has the login credentials or can reset the password or if s/he knows the login credentials of the single-sign-on account associated with it. Finally, we assume the attacker may retrieve the login credentials if there are existing vulnerabilities in the account, e.g. weak password or connections with other accounts. These strong assumptions make the vulnerability analysis more robust, as any countermeasure to these threats is able to cover also other threats with less resources.

At the end of the vulnerability analysis, the reasoner returns a set of countermeasures aimed at reducing the overall risk for the user' accounts. The proposed countermeasures are based on the *single action removal* principle, in which the reasoner evaluates the impact of removing a single step/move from the attacker strategy. Please note that some vulnerabilities are not as easy to remove as others. For example, let us suppose a set of accounts shares the same common password and username. Instead of changing all the passwords, it is more feasible to ensure that the username will never be leaked. Hence, the reasoner provides a *minimum critical set of countermeasures* ensuring that the vulnerabilities are eliminated using as less resources as possible. The minimum critical set is developed using a greedy algorithm. The reasoner provides different set of attack paths, each representing an "or" relation. In other words, for every possible exploit, the reasoner represents each step of the exploit as an element in a set, and the set represents a single exploit. There might be different sets representing the different independent ways an attacker can compromise an account, and the reasoner iteratively selects an element (attack step) that is present in the largest number of sets, until all of the sets are covered [9].

4   Implementation

We have developed a prototype tool to implement the proposed reasoner system. The reasoner is built upon XSB[3] and it includes all the definitions for modelling user details, account details, vulnerabilities, access policies, exploit rules, hypothetical 'what-if' vulnerability analysis as well as to generate countermeasures. We have defined a set of pre-defined Prolog rules, which are built into the reasoner to capture connections across the different accounts, to identify security vulnerabilities, and to define and verify the threat model [22]. Similarly, we have created a set of pre-built queries that can be launched by users to perform attack simulations (e.g., "find out who can access the different accounts"). After performing these queries, the reasoner returns to the user a set of results, namely lists of vulnerable accounts and the steps to perform such attacks. The tool also provides metrics to give a quantitative view of the security status of the list of online accounts. This enables the optimisation of countermeasures and security improvements. For analysing the generated graphs, the proposed system implements the metrics introduced in Sect. 3.3. As a future development, we envision this tool as a standalone application running on the user computer, with a plugin integrated with the browser to interact with the user information (similar to a password manager), as to avoid the user entering the pieces of information manually in the engine. Of course, in this implementation, all the pieces of information need to be securely stored on the user computer and only accessed by the user (similar to a password manager).

4.1   Countermeasures Generation

As recalled previously, the system, after analysing the given accounts together with their vulnerabilities, proposes a set of countermeasures. Once the user has selected some of these countermeasures, the system can be re-run to perform a further analysis to check if further countermeasures should be proposed. For each vulnerability listed in Sect. 3.2, we have defined a set of applicable countermeasures[4], in particular:

- Password related vulnerabilities. When the user is using a bad/weak/common password, or contains publicly available information, the reasoner suggests the user to change the password with a stronger one.

$$countermeas(change, pw) \leftarrow account(X), pwAccount(X, pw),$$
$$(weakPW(pw) \lor badPW(pw) \lor$$
$$commonPW(pw) \lor pubInfoPW(pw)).$$

- Repeated passwords. When the user is using the same password for more than one account, especially when this account is connected or shares the

---

[3] http://xsb.sourceforge.net/.
[4] We give together with the countermeasures their corresponding rules as represented by the reasoner.

same username, the reasoner proposes the user to change the password to a different one.

$$countermeas(change, pw_1) \leftarrow account(X), account(Y), X \neq Y,$$
$$pwAccount(X, pw_1), pwAccount(Y, pw_2),$$
$$(pw_1 = pw_2 \lor similar(pw_1, pw_2)),$$
$$((username(X, U_1), username(X, U_2),$$
$$U_1 = U_2) \lor connected(X, Y)).$$

– Password reset information available publicly or in another account. When a piece of information for resetting a password is publicly available or is available using another account, the reasoner proposes two countermeasures: (i) to change the recovery information, or (ii) to restrict/remove the access to the information needed for resetting the password.

$$countermeas(change, Info) \leftarrow account(X), recovery(X, Info),$$
$$public(Info) \lor (account(Y),$$
$$X \neq Y, inAccount(Y, Info)).$$

$$countermeas(makePrivate, Info) \leftarrow account(X), recovery(X, Info),$$
$$public(Info).$$

5   Preliminary Evaluation of the Framework

We tested our framework by designing a realistic use case in which we have considered all the possible vulnerabilities described in Sect. 3 that an attacker can exploit to access an account. The reasoner was then used to check for possible violations of the policies, and the proposed countermeasures were put in place and a further analysis was performed to verify the effectiveness of the countermeasures in eliminating the vulnerabilities exploited by the attacker.

In detail, we created a set of 35 accounts using the most common online accounts, e.g. Facebook, Twitter, Ebay and Amazon. For each of these websites and social networks, we have modelled their different password strategies realistically, as well as their authentication mechanisms. In addition, for each of the 35 accounts, we have provided user information, e.g. username, email, phone number, and set them as either public or private ones. We have also considered the reset password procedure for each account and the required information: in particular, we have associated those accounts with critical information, such as credit cards details, with stronger passwords than those accounts used in social settings, e.g. public forums. To make the use case more realistic, we have manually inserted some vulnerabilities into the accounts. For example, we have inserted few repetitions of the passwords across accounts as well as minor variations of the same password. Finally, we have also included several relations between different accounts, which mainly arise due to shared login credentials, or recovery email address, or public information used for the recovery.

On this use case, we then have run a what-if vulnerability analysis, where we have used a range of possible types of information available to the attacker. In particular, we have used the following different scenarios: (i) public information, e.g. assuming a username becomes public; (ii) information leaks, when some private pieces of information can be found on leaked database, e.g. of passwords; (iii) website vulnerabilities, e.g. the attacker has access to the account by exploiting a vulnerability of the website. By introducing these vulnerabilities, we then have modelled and evaluated how the amount of information available to an attacker corresponds to changes in the number of exploits and in the number of compromised accounts. As expected, we have seen that rendering some basic pieces of information as public, such as the username or the type of account, is not as critical as disclosing the password of the account in terms of increase in the number of exploitation of accounts. In addition, "information leaks" is the what-if vulnerability scenario with the worse impact for user accounts, as it is the one that brings higher chances for an attacker of successful exploitation. Similarly, when it comes to introducing website vulnerabilities, the impact is very large when introduced in highly interconnected accounts and popular websites. Finally, the evaluation showed that the selection of the countermeasures is targeted on highly interconnected account and on those with a weak password.

6 Conclusion

Securing a large set of interconnected online accounts requires a huge effort from both the users and the service providers. The problem becomes harder when the security policy of one provider can influence or contrast the security policy of another provider. In this paper, we introduced a framework that can be used by users to assess the security and vulnerabilities of their interconnected online accounts. The proposed tool gives a representation of the dependencies between the accounts and proposes countermeasures to ensure their security. As a direction of future research we plan to fully automate the system, e.g. by implementing a browser plugin that securely provides the account information to the reasoner, as well as to increase the number of families of vulnerabilities that can be checked by the reasoner.

Acknowledgments. Erisa Karafili was supported by the European Union's H2020 research and innovation programme under the Marie Skłodowska-Curie grant agreement No 746667. This work builds upon research funded by the Engineering and Physical Sciences Research Council (EPSRC) through grants EP/L022729/1 and EP/N023242/1.

References

1. Ammann, P., Wijesekera, D., Kaushik, S.: Scalable, graph-based network vulnerability analysis. In: Proceedings of the Conference on Computer and Communications Security, pp. 217–224 (2002)

2. Baier, C., Katoen, J.P.: Principles of Model Checking (Representation and Mind Series). The MIT Press (2008)
3. Ben-Meir, E.: Sentry MBA: A Tale of the Most Popular Credential Stuffing Attack Tool (2017). https://blog.cyberint.com/sentry-mba-a-tale-of-the-most-popular-credential-stuffing-attack-tool
4. Bras, T.L.: Online overload - its worse than you thought, July 2015. https://blog.dashlane.com/infographic-online-overload-its-worse-than-you-thought/
5. Data, S.: 100 worst passwords of 2017 (2017). https://s13639.pcdn.co/wp-content/uploads/2017/12/Top-100-Worst-Passwords-of-2017a.pdf
6. Gosling, S.D., Gaddis, S., Vazire, S.: Personality impressions based on Facebook profiles. In: ICWSM (2007)
7. Idika, N., Bhargava, B.: Extending attack graph-based security metrics and aggregating their application. IEEE Trans. Dependable Secure Comput. 9(1), 75–85 (2012)
8. Jajodia, S., Noel, S., O'Berry, B.: Topological analysis of network attack vulnerability. In: Kumar, V., Srivastava, J., Lazarevic, A. (eds.) Managing Cyber Threats. Massive Computing, vol. 5, pp. 247–266. Springer, Boston (2005). https://doi.org/10.1007/0-387-24230-9_9
9. Jha, S., Sheyner, O., Wing, J.: Two formal analyses of attack graphs. In: Proceedings of the Workshop on Computer Security Foundations, pp. 49–63 (2002)
10. Kosinski, M., Stillwell, D., Graepel, T.: Private traits and attributes are predictable from digital records of human behavior. In: Proceedings of the National Academy of Sciences (2013). https://doi.org/10.1073/pnas.1218772110, http://www.pnas.org/content/early/2013/03/06/1218772110
11. Li, W., Vaughn, R.B.: Cluster security research involving the modeling of network exploitations using exploitation graphs. In: 2006 Sixth IEEE International Symposium on Cluster Computing and the Grid, CCGRID 2006, vol. 2, pp. 26–26, May 2006
12. Lippmann, R., et al.: Validating and restoring defense in depth using attack graphs. In: Proceedings of the 2006 IEEE Conference on Military Communications, pp. 981–990. MILCOM 2006. IEEE Press, Piscataway, NJ, USA (2006)
13. Muñoz-González, L., Sgandurra, D., Barrere, M., Lupu, E.C.: Exact inference techniques for the analysis of bayesian attack graphs. IEEE Trans. Dependable Secure Comput. PP(99), 1 (2017). https://doi.org/10.1109/TDSC.2016.2627033
14. Muñoz-González, L., Sgandurra, D., Paudice, A., Lupu, E.C.: Efficient attack graph analysis through approximate inference. ACM Trans. Priv. Secur. 20(3), 10:1–10:30 (2017). https://doi.org/10.1145/3105760
15. Ortalo, R., Deswarte, Y., Kaâniche, M.: Experimenting with quantitative evaluation tools for monitoring operational security. IEEE Trans. Softw. Eng. 25(5), 633–650 (1999)
16. Ou, X., Boyer, W., McQueen, M.: A scalable approach to attack graph generation. In: Proceedings of ACM Conference on Computer and Communications Security, pp. 336–345 (2006)
17. Ou, X., Govindavajhala, S., Appel, A.W.: MulVAL: a logic-based network security analyzer. In: Proceedings of the 14th Conference on USENIX Security Symposium - Volume 14, SSYM 2005, p. 8. USENIX Association, Berkeley, CA, USA (2005)
18. Pepitone, J.: Hack attack exposes major gap in Amazon and Apple security, August 2012. http://money.cnn.com/2012/08/07/technology/mat-honan-hacked/
19. Poolsappasit, N., Dewri, R., Ray, I.: Dynamic security risk management using Bayesian attack graphs. IEEE Trans. Dependable Secure Comput. 9(1), 61–74 (2012)

20. Rabkin, A.: Personal knowledge questions for fallback authentication: security questions in the era of Facebook. In: Proceedings of the 4th Symposium on Usable Privacy and Security, SOUPS 2008, pp. 13–23. ACM, New York (2008)
21. Ritchey, R.W., Ammann, P.: Using model checking to analyze network vulnerabilities. In: Proceeding of 2000 IEEE Symposium on Security and Privacy, S P 2000, pp. 156–165 (2000)
22. Sgandurra, D., Karafili, E., Lupu, E.: Formalizing threat models for virtualized systems. In: Ranise, S., Swarup, V. (eds.) Data and Applications Security and Privacy XXX, pp. 251–267. Springer International Publishing, Cham (2016). https://doi.org/10.1007/978-3-319-41483-6_18
23. Sheyner, O., Haines, J., Jha, S., Lippmann, R., Wing, J.: Automated generation and analysis of attack graphs. In: Proceedings of the IEEE Symposium on Security and Privacy, pp. 273–284 (2002)
24. Sheyner, O., Wing, J.: Tools for generating and analyzing attack graphs. In: de Boer, F.S., Bonsangue, M.M., Graf, S., de Roever, W.-P. (eds.) FMCO 2003. LNCS, vol. 3188, pp. 344–371. Springer, Heidelberg (2004). https://doi.org/10.1007/978-3-540-30101-1_17

Towards a Framework for Testing the Security of IoT Devices Consistently

Gurjan Lally[1,2(✉)] and Daniele Sgandurra[2]

[1] Department of Computer Science, Royal Holloway, University of London,
Egham, UK
gurjan.lally.2015@live.rhul.ac.uk
[2] Information Security Group, Royal Holloway, University of London,
Egham, UK
daniele.sgandurra@rhul.ac.uk

Abstract. The Internet of Things (IoT) permeates society in many areas, such as automotive, smart-homes, smart-cities, healthcare, and critical infrastructures. Even if the IoT promises economic growth as well as convenience for users, the security (and safety) implications of the IoT are equally significant. In fact, weak security in IoT devices could have dangerous consequences, such as to a car crash, or an intruder entering in our home. As an example, in October 2016, the distributed denial of service attack on Dyn, a company controlling and managing several DNS services, brought down most of America's Internet, and was caused by an IoT botnet (Mirai). This is mainly due to an increasing number of vulnerabilities in IoT devices being discovered on a daily basis, and that are the consequence of poor IoT security practices. To properly address the security and testing of IoT devices, the first step is the description of a threat model. However, few IoT manufactures base their testing on sound threat modelling techniques and comprehensive IoT security guidelines.

For these reasons, in this paper we propose a methodological approach for IoT security testing, which extends the OWASP IoT framework to include threat models to guide the selection of tests used to evaluate IoT attack surfaces and associated vulnerabilities. In addition, the proposed extended framework includes indications on how to actually test a given vulnerability and a set of recommended tools for performing the tests. To this end, we have devised a set of procedures associated with the tests, e.g. accessing device hardware or resetting the device. We also describe a set of tests based on the framework we have performed on IoT devices to test their security. In particular, we have tested the framework on a home router, a relatively cheap baby monitor, and a pricey security system. The methodological testing of the devices reported that the baby monitor showed signs of inadequate security, the router patching any known vulnerabilities as expected from a well-known manufacturer, and the security system quashing any penetration testing attempts.

Keywords: Internet of Things · OWASP · Attack surfaces
Testing methodology

© Springer Nature Switzerland AG 2018
A. Saracino and P. Mori (Eds.): ETAA 2018, LNCS 11263, pp. 88–102, 2018.
https://doi.org/10.1007/978-3-030-04372-8_8

1 Introduction

As defined in [13], the Internet of Things (IoT) is "a system of interrelated computing devices, mechanical and digital machines, objects, animals, or people that are provided with unique identifiers and the ability to transfer data over a network without requiring human-to-human or human-to-computer interaction". The IoT encompasses a large range of devices ('things'), among which every-day household electronics, such as dishwashers, fridges, smart cameras, smart watches, smart glasses, smart TVs, and smart light bulbs. Wearable devices can monitor heart rate, steps, and spent calories to name just a few 'smart' features introduced by IoT devices. The IoT offers almost limitless possibilities of positive features, finally fulfilling at least some of the alacritous visions of futurists in the mid to late twentieth century[1]. These positives are hard to outweigh, but negatives do exist. Concerns over data collection by product manufacturers and associated privacy, as well as security vulnerabilities in these devices, might well not be enough to completely put people off using IoT devices or care for these issues [9], but these concerns are still prominent.

Perhaps the most nefarious use of IoT devices is the one performed by botnets. One in particular, the Mirai botnet [11], exploits something as simple as default credentials in IoT devices, gaining root access to recruit infected devices to the botnet. This particular botnet made global headlines after causing massive Internet outages, mainly in America. Articles highlighted the root cause being infected IoT devices, stirring skepticism over these devices as a whole. The botnet code itself uses a list of known default credentials for different devices and brute-forces IoT devices over the Telnet protocol. This is a shockingly simple exploitation of IoT devices, yet very common nowadays. The first question is why the Telnet protocol is used so frequently, as the protocol is very well known to be insecure by transmitting data in the clear. Devices are often manufactured with trivial hard coded credentials in firmware, such as username 'admin' and password 'admin'. More complex hard coded credentials still pose a problem, since they could be extracted from the device firmware. For example, the main manufacturer whose devices were targeted by the Mirai botnet simply changed their mechanism of default credentials by assigning a default username and password, stored in a table in the firmware, for each day of the year [16]. Such a fix is clearly not adequate – a method of setting user credentials upon first boot would make more sense (but this would bring other usability issues). Of course, default credentials and firmware extraction/analysis are just examples of vulnerabilities related to attack surfaces. In fact, most of IoT devices for everyday consumers are still not designed with security in mind, with a reported one out of ten devices displaying the prevalent issue of common default credentials alone [10]. Only few manufacturers have started to include security practices in IoT design and development, mainly due to the publicity around the concept of the exploitation of an IoT device potentially having a direct impact on consumers and negative press [14, 15].

---

[1] https://www.postscapes.com/internet-of-things-history/.

For these reasons, we propose an extension to the OWASP IoT attack surface mappings [12] with the aim of making the security testing of IoT devices more rigorous as to significantly reduce their number of vulnerabilities. In particular, we have extended the OWASP framework to include: (i) a mapping of vulnerabilities to a set of security tests – to facilitate the selection of tests to be performed; (ii) a mapping of tests to potentially useful tools to perform the test – to guide users/manufacturers on the choice of the tools to perform the test; and (iii) a more detailed threat modelling – to formalize under which assumptions and scenarios the tests are meaningful. The main aim of the proposed framework is to allow IoT designers, as well as manufactures and end-users, to model and risk-assess IoT security in a methodological and comprehensive way. To evaluate the efficacy of the proposed framework, we have used it to guide the tests on three classes of IoT devices.

The paper is structured as follows. In Sect. 2, we describe related works. In Sect. 3, we firstly briefly recall the main concepts of the IoT OWASP framework, and we then describe the proposed changes to the IoT OWASP framework, by discussing the extended surface mapping to include IoT security considerations, the tools to use and threat models. In Sect. 4, we report the results of the tests performed on three classes of IoT devices by following the proposed testing methodology, and we discuss our findings. Finally, in Sect. 5 we conclude the paper.

2   Related Works

In [1], the authors have analysed the security of Samsung's SmartThings platform and found several security vulnerabilities. Similarly, in [2] the authors have performed functionality extension attacks on IoT devices using smart-lights as a covert Li-Fi communication system to get data from a highly secure office building. The authors were able to read the leaked data from a distance of over 100 m using cheap equipment. The authors of [3] have designed a feature-distributed malware to perform various malicious activities, such as unlocking smart-locks and disarming security alarms. These results show that traditional web attack techniques, such as cookie stealing, can be turned into sophisticated attacks on IoT devices. Similarly, the authors of [4] examine the security of five commercial home smart-locks, and show that most of these devices suffer from poor design and implementation choices. [5] analyses the IoT vulnerabilities from insecure web/mobile/cloud interfaces, by testing insufficient authentication and authorization, insecure network services, lack of transport encryption and integrity verification, privacy concerns, insufficient security configurability, insecure software/firmware, and poor physical security. In [6] the authors examine the security of different categories of IoT devices to understand their resilience under different threat models, in particular physical access and close proximity of the attacker. However, none of these papers has proposed a framework to enable IoT manufacturers to test the security of IoT devices methodically by using different tools and security assumptions [7, 8], which is the main goal of this paper.

3   Proposed Extended IoT Framework

This section involves the analysis of relevant IoT attack surfaces and vulnerabilities from IoT OWASP framework, and then it proposes an extension to include testing considerations, tools, and threat models for each vulnerability.

3.1   IoT Threat Modelling

A critical aspect of security testing is to evaluate all possible attack surfaces and their associated vulnerabilities, and then select specific attack surfaces to analyze and test. In IoT scenarios, attack surfaces are points of an IoT device at which an attacker can gain access to it to perform a security violation, e.g. by delivering a malicious payload. Vulnerabilities are the means by which an attack can be performed. As an example, Table 1 lists some of the attack surfaces and associate vulnerabilities from the OWASP IoT Framework [12].

Table 1. IoT OWASP framework (excerpt)

Attack Surface	Vulnerabilities	
Ecosystem access control	• Implicit trust between components • Enrolment security	• Decommissioning system • Lost access procedures
Device memory	• Cleartext usernames • Cleartext passwords	• Third-party credentials • Encryption keys
Device physical interfaces	• Firmware extraction • User CLI • Admin CLI	• Privilege escalation • Reset to insecure state • Removal of storage media
Device web interface	• SQL injection • Cross-site scripting • Cross-site Request Forgery • Username enumeration	• Weak passwords • Account lockout • Known default credentials

It appears evident that, while the OWASP framework includes several attack surfaces and sets of vulnerabilities, there are no indications on how to actually test these vulnerabilities, and under which security condition(s). Therefore, the first requirement (R1) of our methodological approach to testing the devices is to identify *suitable* attack surfaces, based on factors such as knowledge of the scenario (i.e., threat model), and whether the attack surface is suitable to the device being tested. For example, prematurely choosing the Device Web Interface attack surface to test would not make sense on a device with no web interface. The second requirement (R2) of our framework is to provide a set of guidelines describing how to test the vulnerabilities along with the list of tools that can be used to perform the test. The aim of these requirements is to make the framework more rigorous and to facilitate the selection of tests to be performed.

3.2   Extended Attack Surface Mapping

To consider these two requirements, the extended framework includes three additional mappings for each vulnerability, which are:

(i) *IoT Security Considerations*, i.e. guidelines on how to perform the testing;
(ii) *Methodologies and Tools*, i.e. a list of suggested tools and methodologies to perform the tests;
(iii) *Threat Models*, i.e. a description of the security assumptions, in particular in terms of attacker's access;

The first requirement (R1) is satisfied by including in the framework *IoT Security Considerations* and *Methodologies and Testing tools*. The first extension describes effectively means of testing, that is, the ways in which to test a given vulnerability if it seems possible. The second extension, *Methodologies and Tools,* refers to various pieces of software or hardware, as well as methodologies, that can be used to perform the testing process. This piece of information is useful to testers, since it works in concurrency with the Security Considerations to extend upon what will be needed to actually test the vulnerability. The second requirement (R2) is satisfied by extending the framework to include *Threat Models*. In fact, some vulnerabilities may require hardware access, and some may be exploited remotely. The extension *Threat Models* defines the security assumptions, e.g. proximity of attacker to perform the attack, so that manufactures can decide whether to perform the testing or not based on the device deployment scenarios. For instance, in case a device is not deployed in open fields, all the tests related to physical attacks could be omitted.

We have included these threat models in the extended framework

- **Physical access**, i.e. an attacker that can tamper with the hardware;
- **Close access**, i.e. an attacker that is in close proximity of the IoT device (e.g., RFID access), without having physical access;
- **Network access**, in an attacker able to get access to the same network of the IoT device (e.g., WiFi);
- **Remote access**, i.e. an attacker able to connect remotely to the device;
- **Application access**, i.e. an attacker able to connect remotely to the application (typically running on a smartphone) that controls the IoT device;
- **Router/Hub access**, i.e. an attacker able to connect remotely to the home router or hub mediating/controlling the IoT device;
- **Cloud access**, i.e. an attacker able to connect to the Cloud backend only.

Each of these accesses is associated with a set of attacks that an attacker can perform, and a stronger assumption (e.g., physical access), which also includes the attacks associated with a weaker assumption (e.g., network access), while the vice-versa is not true. The symbols we have used to visually represent these threat models are shown in Table 2.

Table 2. Symbols used in the framework to represent the threat models

Physical Access	Close Access	Network Access	Remote Access	App Access	Gateway Access	Cloud Access
📷	((•))	📶	🌐	📱	📡	☁

Table 3 reports the proposed extended framework by showing a representative subset of the vulnerabilities and attack areas for which we have provided an extension, namely *Device Physical Interfaces*, *Device Web Interface*, *Device Firmware*, *Device Network Services*, and *Local Data Storage*[2].

As already recalled, by selecting a specific *Threat Model*, the proposed framework shows the vulnerabilities to test belonging to the uncovered attack surfaces. Then, the associated *IoT Security Considerations* report a set of guidelines on how to perform the testing. For example, in the *Physical Access* threat model, the *Device Physical Interfaces Attack Surface* is enabled. Here, a possible vulnerability is *Firmware Extraction*, and one of the main *Security Consideration* is that access to serial ports from hardware must be tested, and a set of *Methodologies and Tools* to obtain the firmware are described.

In the following section we describe how we have used the extended framework to assess the security of three categories of IoT devices.

4   Testing with the Extended Framework

This section covers the actual testing and describes the results obtained following the extended IoT framework. In detail, we have tested the devices on a router, on a baby monitor, and on a security system. For the sake of responsible disclosure, we omit the details of the manufacturers and IoT models of any of these devices, and any details which could lead to any harmful outcome.

A preliminary phase of the proposed methodological approach taken to the testing is that of *reconnaissance*, which involves learning about and gathering information on the target before the test. In our tests, for each of the three devices, the following pieces information were gathered: chipsets used, known vulnerabilities (to verify their existence or absence), information on how open the devices, as well as other various specifics that would aid the testing. In one case, to speed up the testing, firmware for one of the devices was obtained by emailing the manufacturer and having them send the actual binary.

---

[2] For the sake of conciseness, the Table shown here briefly summarizes "IoT Security Considerations" and "Methodologies and Tools".

Table 3. Proposed extended OWASP IoT attack surface areas.

Device Physical Interfaces	Device Web Interface	Device Firmware	Device Network Services	Local Data Storage

Vulnerability	IoT Security Considerations (How to Test)	Methodologies and Tools	Threat Model
Firmware extraction	Gain access to serial ports from hardware and dump firmware	(physical) UART to USB cables	
User/admin CLI	Use potential serial ports to access the CLI	(physical) UART to USB into computer	
Privilege escalation	Potential buffer overflow attacks, command injections	Metasploit framework	
Reset to insecure state	Reset button? Analyse network activity thereafter	Wireshark	
Known default credentials	Check internet for known default password lists for a given device	Browsing internet	
SQL injection	Give malicious input in some form on the web interface	SQL ninja/Metasploit SQLi tools	
Weak passwords	Guess passwords or bruteforce	Brutus bruteforcer	
Account lockout	Test whether account locks by constantly logging in incorrectly	Brutus or manually	
Username enumeration	Bruteforce default usernames until some message indicates its existence	Brutus or any Metasploit bruteforcer	
Hardcoded credentials	Extract the firmware and manually analyse it for any credentials	Binwalk firmware extraction and analysis tool	
Sensitive information disclosure	Same as above, but analyse for sensitive information instead	Binwalk firmware extraction and analysis tool	
Sensitive URL disclosure	Same as above, but look for any sensitive URLs	Binwalk firmware extraction and analysis tool	
Firmware version display and/or last update date	Displayed in some UI? Transmitted over network?	Wireshark	
Information disclosure	Intercept packets to gain unintended information	Wireshark	
Administrative command line	Check an open port (Telnet or SSH). Guess default credentials, bruteforce or extract firmware as above	Fing network service identifier to identify Telnet/SSH. Firmware tools as above	
Injection	Inject code into network messages/user input, perform dot traversal	Metasploit tools	
Denial of service	Flood a device with network traffic/packets/broken packets	Ettercap	
Vulnerable UDP services	Sending spoofed IP UDP packets or even DoS attacks on open UDP ports	Ettercap DoS	
Unencrypted services	Read unencrypted data with a packet sniffer	Wireshark	
Unencrypted data	View data perhaps stored by applications accompanying the device	Dex2jar for APK to JAR	
Update sent without encryption	Look for streams of unencrypted packets related to an update	Wireshark	
No Manual update mechanism	Look for ways by which it is not possible to manually update	Web interfaces	

4.1 Selecting Suitable Vulnerabilities from the Extended Framework

After the reconnaissance phase, vulnerabilities to be tested for each device are carefully selected based on the threat model and on whether a specific vulnerability would be suitable for that device. The list of vulnerabilities considered in our tests is shown in Table 4, and will be detailed in the following.

Table 4. Tested vulnerabilities for each device. R denotes router, B denotes baby monitor camera, S denotes the security System.

Attack Surface	Vulnerability	R	B	S
Device network services	Information disclosure	X	X	X
	Administrative command line	X	X	X
	Denial of service		X	X
	Unencrypted services		X	X
Device web interface	Account lockout	X		X
	Weak passwords	X		
	SQL injection	X		
	Default known credentials	X		
Update mechanism	Update sent without encryption	X		
Device physical interface	User/admin CLI		X	
	Firmware extraction		X	
Device firmware	Hardcoded credentials		X	X
	Firmware version display	X	X	X
	Firmware last update date	X	X	X

4.2 Home Router Testing

In the considered testbed, the home router is one that has previously been tested by security professionals, and a well-known reported vulnerability with this specific device is the use of default credentials, with the username and password being 'admin'. Therefore, we first started with security testing of credentials. The expectation would be for this vulnerability to have been fixed, despite the issue still being listed on a frequently update website of default credentials. Following the list of guidelines in the extended framework, we performed the tests through the automatic testing of credentials on the web interface, and easily-guessed credentials were not being an issue anymore. We then tested possible vulnerabilities to the firmware and update mechanism. Upon actually setting up the device and connecting to the router, a prompt was made by a webpage to run a firmware update in order for the device to work. However, this was easily skipped past by closing the webpage. One could then proceed to use the device normally, potentially postponing the firmware update indefinitely, as a common user would, resulting in any possible vulnerability patches in the update being left unapplied. However, to access the router login page, the firmware had to be updated. Even so, it should not be allowed to be possible to skip a crucial firmware update and use the device. An incoming update to the router was intercepted, using Wireshark[3].

---

[3] https://www.wireshark.org/.

The contents were encrypted, meaning that the device is secure against the Update Sent Without Encryption vulnerability, listed under the Update Mechanism attack surface.

We then tested for an administrative command line as outlined by the Device Network Services attack surface mappings. As per the Security Considerations for the vulnerability, open service ports were searched for to potentially gain access to a command line interface (CLI). The aim is to establish an SSH or Telnet connection. To do this, Fing service scanner[4] and the Netstat[5] command was used. The router had a lot of miscellaneous ports open, but none which could potentially hold the route to a CLI. It turns out that it could actually be chosen to enable remote connection to the router on the router settings page by enabling SSH. Had there been an accessible administrative command line available over the network, this would have been a further venue of possible exploitation to test. The Web interface was tested further with malicious input into the username and password fields. Following the recommendations reported on the *Tools* column, we used SQL ninja[6] to perform an SQL injection, which did not return any successful result. We discovered that the router obtained credentials from a cloud service and that the manufacturer has taken measures against SQL injections – noted as the most important web application security risk [13]. By this same method of testing suggested by the framework, we also discovered that the web interface employs account lockout. In addition, weak (default) passwords could not be tested for, since the user has to set the password on the admin page. The final test was for Information Disclosure vulnerability. This test returned positive as some sensitive information was disclosed. In particular, by using Wireshark (See footnote 3) to analyze packets, upon loading the device web interface, it was observed that details of the device were sent over HTTP in the clear (see Fig. 1). This includes a display of the current firmware

```
},
{
"deviceID": "                                    ",
"lastChangeRevision": 1,
"model": {
"deviceType": "Infrastructure",
"manufacturer": "               ",
"modelNumber": "            ",
"hardwareVersion": "2",
"description": "                  Wireless-          Router"
},
"unit": {
"serialNumber": "            ",
"firmwareVersion": "           ",
"firmwareDate": "            "
},
```

Fig. 1. Cleartext device details

---

[4] https://www.fing.io/.

[5] https://linux.die.net/man/8/netstat.

[6] http://sqlninja.sourceforge.net/.

version and its last update, as well as the serial number. This information is only sent when loading the web interface.

It is a more threating outcome when the user actually logs into the web interface as all user information and device information, including the device's password, is transmitted in clear text (see Fig. 2). Hence, adversaries could simply just read the HTTP packet and have access to sensitive information, such as password – which can also be reused across other accounts of the same user.

```
48,
],
"supportedWideChannels": [
0,
36,
40,
44,
48
],
"supportedSecurityTypes": [
"None",
"WEP",
"WPA2-Personal",
"WPA2-Enterprise",
"WPA-Mixed-Personal",
],
"maxRadiusSharedKeyLength": 64,
"settings": {
"isEnabled": true,
"mode": "802.11mixed",
"ssid": "תקשורת",
"broadcastSSID": true,
"channelWidth": "Auto",
"channel": 0,
"security": "WPA2-Personal",
"wpaPersonalSettings": {
"passphrase": "סיסמה"
}
```

Fig. 2. Cleartext credentials details

4.3 Baby Monitor Testing

The Baby monitor we have tested is a low-cost baby monitor, designed to send a video stream to an application on a mobile phone with the camera registered to it. It does not have a web link available to view the video, but only a mobile application.

The entire initial setup phase of the device and its controlling application had secure network communications, which involved user details input to the application, entering wireless network details, and configuring the two devices such that the mobile application displayed the camera's live video feed. Any information disclosure here and subsequently through any future communications was not evident during the testing. All communications were encrypted, and no details were transmitted in the clear. To test possible vulnerabilities here, following the framework guidelines, Wireshark was used as well as an Android application titled 'Packet Capture'[7], which records packets

---

[7] https://play.google.com/store/apps/details?id=app.greyshirts.sslcapture.

in and out of a smartphone for a set period of time. Packets were then individually analyzed, in particular around 90 packets during the camera initialization and 20–50 for each following analysis of general camera usage.

As per the extended framework, Fing network service scanner (See footnote 4) was then used to scan for any open services with the hope of finding a service that would offer access to some administrative CLI. One service detected of particular interest was Telnet, which is dangerous, since it transmits data in clear-text. The camera had an open Telnet port indeed, requiring credentials to connect to, and so a dictionary attack could be performed. It seemed appropriate to gather some further understanding of the device to do this. Since the camera's firmware was not readily available anywhere on the Internet, we followed the framework guidelines on how to exploit the APK of the camera's mobile application. In fact, the APK includes the compiled version of the Java source code for a mobile application, which still embeds some strings from the original source code. To this end, as per the framework guidelines, we have analyzed the APK with automatic tools to search for words such as 'default', 'Telnet', 'pass', 'user', as well as any variations of these words including capital letters. There were lots of instances of these words in the code but after following the program control flow of these instances, we discovered that no code referred to the Telnet login. There was an imported class used, 'Telnet login', and a default Apache library class but both classes were not actually used in the product. One interesting finding, however, was that the actual camera was manufactured by one of manufacturers that produced several vulnerable devices targeted by the Mirai botnet for default credentials. The framework includes guidelines on to perform a dictionary attack, which we did on the Telnet login of the camera with the Mirai word list, as well as any other common logins by using some MSFconsole[8] commands. However, the tests were unsuccessful and username enumeration was not possible. The connection was also dropped after several attempts and 60 s. Similarly, brute-forcing the Telnet port would take a very long time without meaningful results.

We then considered the security of the device's firmware. The firmware version and update-date was clearly listed on the application. To access the firmware by referencing our framework, it made sense to pursue the Device Physical Interface Attack Surface. IoT Security considerations were taken into account for the Firmware Extraction vulnerability, and it was quickly learned that hardware would need to be dismantled to access useful serial ports. Additionally, as per the recommended Tools to test for the vulnerability, UART to USB cables were required. After emailing the manufacturer and obtaining the cables, it was learned that, to access the camera's hardware, the device would need to be broken open with the risk of damaging the hardware to the point of it not working again. The device was opened, with the goal of finding a UART serial port (see Fig. 3), which might have offered access to an administrative CLI as well as the firmware for the device if connected to.

Upon analysis of the hardware, we found a candidate for a UART pinout, which we tested with a voltmeter to read the voltages given off by each port, so that could be detected whether it was a UART pinout based on the voltage given off by each port and

---

[8] https://www.offensive-security.com/metasploit-unleashed/msfconsole/.

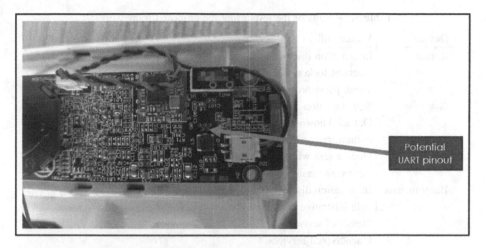

Fig. 3. Potential UART pinout on baby monitor camera

their voltages relative to each-other. The voltages were far too close together to be UART pins – it was expected that there would be a fixed amount of voltage between them, relative to each-other but this was not evident.

The final test on this device was to understand its resilience against DoS attacks. After referencing the framework, attempts were made to take down the camera by flooding it with a stream of packets, as per the Security Considerations for the Denial of Service vulnerability. To do this, Ettercap[9], a program shipped with Kali Linux[10], was used as listed in the extended framework. By specifying the IP address and the type of attack to carry out, Ettercap proceeded to transmit to the device an overwhelming number packets. The device physically heated up and its light flickered red indicating an error. The video stream then slowly flickered out through packet loss and the camera turned itself off. Hence, the DoS attack was performed successfully.

4.4 Security System Testing

The final IoT device that we tested is a reputable security system, complete with motion detection, Cloud-stored video recordings, two-way camera communication and support for multiple cameras. The camera streams to a website which requires a user login to connect to the camera. The device web interface was regarded as secure: SQL injections failed and account lockouts were enabled. Additionally, weak passwords were not permitted for the device, and all the efforts at analyzing the web interface were unsuccessful. Regarding the Device Network Services Attack Surface, any network communications were encrypted, and so no information was retrieved. Similarly, there were no publicly accessible ports on the device. Our preliminary tests showed that this device was designed with security in mind, considering the selected attack surfaces-vulnerabilities pair.

---

[9] https://www.ettercap-project.org/.
[10] https://www.kali.org/.

Table 5. Results of the tests using the proposed framework.

Device	Vulnerability	Vulnerability exploited?
Router	Information disclosure	Y
	Account lockout	N
	Weak passwords	N
	SQL injection	N
	Default known credentials	N
	Administrative command line	N
	Update sent without encryption	–
	Firmware version display/update date	Y
Baby monitor	Information disclosure	N
	Administrative command line	?
	Denial of service	Y
	Unencrypted services	N
	Firmware extraction	N
	User/admin CLI	?
	Hardcoded credentials	?
	Firmware version display/update date	Y
Secure system	Information disclosure	N
	Administrative command line	?
	Denial of services	–
	Hardcoded credentials	N
	Unencrypted services	N
	Firmware version display/last update date	–
	Account lockout	N
	Weak passwords	N
	SQL injection	N
	Known default credentials	N

4.5   Results of the Testing

The results of the tests are shown in Table 5, which reports, for each device, the vulnerabilities tested, and whether or not the vulnerability was realized. Here, 'Y' denotes realization, 'N' denotes that the vulnerability was not realized, '-' denotes untested, and '?' indicates there could potentially be an issue with more tests.

By following the framework guidelines, we discovered that the results of the tests were different than expected. For example, it was not expected that the router would have basic security issues such as instances of clear text communication. Additionally, it was not expected that the baby monitor camera would be as secure as it was, despite few existing issues. We expected to find some information disclosure or problems with network communications at least, but there was nothing in that sense. An expected result, however, was the security system device's firm security against the attack vectors chosen. Therefore, it appeared that the device is properly designed from a security perspective – at least, considering the five selected attack surfaces.

5 Conclusion

IoT security is still an issue today, in particular as several insecure devices are still mass produced, with little attention from manufacturers on device security. However, with IoT regulation groups and boards aimed at ensuring that security standards are kept – e.g. the EU IoT Council[11] – we probably should see a swing in a positive direction for the security of IoT devices. Existing frameworks to test IoT devices simply are not mature enough for testers. There definitely needs to be an extension to it both in terms of what is included, e.g. the extension of tools/attack scope, as well as more vulnerabilities being added, such as relay/replay attacks. IoT security frameworks also need constant updating: for example, the OWASP attack surfaces mapping page was last updated in 2015, which is not in line with how IoT has developed since then.

This paper shows that the proposed extension to the OWASP attack surface to vulnerabilities mappings is useful from a testing perspective. In particular, the testing methodology we have proposed adds further structure to the process of identifying and exploiting any vulnerability in IoT devices and would be useful to actually add to the OWASP IoT attack surface mappings. A future extension to our proposed framework, which we are currently working on, is the addendum of extended mappings for the remaining attack surfaces listed in the original OWASP framework.

Acknowledgment. This work was partially supported by the European Union's Horizon 2020 research and innovation programme under grant agreement No 779391 (FutureTPM).

References

1. Fernandes, E., Jung, J., Prakash, A.: Security analysis of emerging smart home applications. In: 2016 IEEE Symposium on Security and Privacy (SP), pp. 636–654. IEEE (2016)
2. Ronen, E., Shamir, A.: Extended functionality attacks on IoT devices: the case of smart lights. In: 2016 IEEE European Symposium on Security and Privacy (EuroS&P), pp. 3–12. IEEE (2016)
3. Min, B., Varadharajan, V.: Design and evaluation of feature distributed malware attacks against the Internet of Things (IoT). In: 2015 20th International Conference on Engineering of Complex Computer Systems (ICECCS), pp. 80–89. IEEE (2015)
4. Ho, G., Leung, D., Mishra, P., Hosseini, A., Song, D., Wagner, D.: Smart locks: lessons for securing commodity Internet of Things devices. In: Proceedings of the 11th ACM on Asia conference on Computer and Communications Security, pp. 461–472. ACM (2016)
5. Bertino, E., Islam, N.: Botnets and internet of things security. Computer **2**, 76–79 (2017)
6. Xu, H., Sgandurra, D., Mayes, K., Li, P., Wang, R.: Analysing the resilience of the internet of things against physical and proximity attacks. In: Wang, G., Atiquzzaman, M., Yan, Z., Choo, K.-K.R. (eds.) SpaCCS 2017. LNCS, vol. 10658, pp. 291–301. Springer, Cham (2017). https://doi.org/10.1007/978-3-319-72395-2_27
7. Sgandurra, D., Lupu, E.: Evolution of attacks, threat models, and solutions for virtualized systems. ACM Comput. Surv. (CSUR) **48**(3), 46 (2016)

---

[11] https://www.theinternetofthings.eu/.

8. Sgandurra, D., Karafili, E., Lupu, E.: Formalizing threat models for virtualized systems. In: Ranise, S., Swarup, V. (eds.) DBSec 2016. LNCS, vol. 9766, pp. 251–267. Springer, Cham (2016). https://doi.org/10.1007/978-3-319-41483-6_18
9. Rouffineau, T.: Consumers are terrible at updating their connected devices (2016). https://blog.ubuntu.com/2016/12/15/research-consumers-are-terrible-at-updating-their-connected-devices
10. Shipulin, K.: Practical ways to misuse a router. Positive Technologies (2017). http://blog.ptsecurity.com/2017/06/practical-ways-to-misuse-router.html
11. Antonakakis, M., et al.: Understanding the mirai botnet. In: USENIX Security Symposium, pp. 1092–1110 (2017)
12. OWASP: IoT attack surface areas (2015). https://www.owasp.org/index.php/IoT_Attack_Surface_areas
13. OWASP: Top 10 2017: The Ten Most Critical Web Application Security Risks. Sl: The OWASP Foundation (2013)
14. Trendall, S.: Labour MP: if a device is called 'smart' – don't buy it. PublicTechnology.net (2018). https://publictechnology.net/articles/news/labour-mp-if-device-called-%E2%80%98smart%E2%80%99-%E2%80%93-don%E2%80%99t-buy-it
15. Ranger, S.: Internet of Things: finding a way out of the security nightmare. ZDNet (2016). https://www.zdnet.com/article/internet-of-things-finding-a-way-out-of-the-security-nightmare/
16. Paul: Mirai Redux: a year's worth of DVR passwords published online. The Security Ledger (2017). https://securityledger.com/2017/01/mirai-redux-a-years-worth-of-dvr-passwords-published-online/

Misuse Detection in a Simulated IaaS Environment

Burhan Al-Bayati[1,2], Nathan Clarke[1,3(✉)], Paul Dowland[3(✉)],
and Fudong Li[1,4(✉)]

[1] Centre for Security, Communications and Network Research, Plymouth
University, Plymouth, UK
{burhan.al-bayati,n.clarke,fudong.li}@plymouth.ac.uk
[2] Computer Science Department, College Science,
Diyala University, Diyala, Iraq
[3] Security Research Institute, Edith Cowan University, Perth, WA, Australia
p.dowland@plymouth.ac.uk
[4] School of Computing, University of Portsmouth, Portsmouth, UK

Abstract. Cloud computing is an emerging technology paradigm by offering elastic computing resources for individuals and organisations with low cost. However, security is still the most sensitive issue in cloud computing services as the service remains accessible to anyone after initial simple authentication login for significant periods. This has led to increase vulnerability to potential attacks and sensitive customer information being misused. To be able to detect this misuse, an additional intelligent security measures are arguably required. Tracking user's activity by building user behaviour profiles is one technique that has been successfully applied in a variety of applications such as telecommunication misuse and credit card fraud. This paper presents an investigation into applying behavioural profiling in a simulated IaaS-based infrastructure for the purposes of misuse detection by verifying the active user continuously and transparently. In order to examine the feasibility of this approach within cloud infrastructure services, a private dataset was collected containing real interactions of 60 users over a three-week period (totalling 1,048,195 log entries). A series of experiments were conducted using supervised machine learning algorithms to examine the ability of detecting abnormal usage. The best experimental result of 0.32% Equal Error Rate is encouraging and indicates the ability of identifying misuse within cloud computing services via the behavioural profiling technique.

Keywords: Continuous identity verification · Misuse
Behavioural profiling · IaaS · Cloud computing services

1 Introduction

According to the Cisco Global Cloud Index, by 2019, more than 80% of all data centre traffic will be cloud traffic, and around 86% of all amount of processing will be achieved in cloud infrastructure services [1]. Moreover, cloud Infrastructure as a Service (IaaS) is a vital underlying infrastructure model that supports all other cloud

© Springer Nature Switzerland AG 2018
A. Saracino and P. Mori (Eds.): ETAA 2018, LNCS 11263, pp. 103–115, 2018.
https://doi.org/10.1007/978-3-030-04372-8_9

services. However, IaaS was reported as the most vulnerable cloud model [2]. As a result, customers would have concerns about unauthorised access to their information that is remotely managed in these services.

Due to the online nature of those services, authentication provides the primary security control to prevent misuse by relying upon point-of-entry based passwords. By stealing customers' login credentials, hackers can gain illicit access and misuse the service and user information. Many incidents have targeted popular cloud computing service providers, for example:

- According to Cloud Security Alliance, a number of security incidents occurred to a British telecom provider (TalkTalk) in 2014 and 2015, resulted in disclosing four million of their customers' personal information [3].
- The Microsoft Azure cloud computing platform faced a serious security incidents in March 2009, led to a massive collapse and outage of the service for 22 h, with a loss of 45% of user data [4].
- Dropbox was hacked in July 2012; usernames and passwords of many users were stolen from third-party websites; these stolen credentials helped hackers to get access successfully to customers' accounts and misused their data [5].
- Apple iCloud was compromised in 2014 as more than 20,000 passwords of its customer accounts were stolen, resulting in user's personal photographs, specifically celebrities, being leaked online [6].
- Google's Gmail server faced attack in 2016; more than 272 million email addresses and passwords were stolen [7].

It is clear from these incidents that users' sensitive information within cloud computing services can be abused by cybercriminals even though security controls were in place and dedicated security teams were allocated. Therefore, additional security techniques are required to protect cloud services from being compromised and misused. This paper proposes a novel continuous identity verification system as a solution to protect cloud infrastructure service by operating transparently to detect abnormal access. Behavioural profiling can provide a continuous and transparent assessing user's identity while they interact with cloud services. By creating user behaviour profiles, it can be identified people based upon the way in which they interact with cloud computing services. Therefore, the current user's activities (e.g. time of opening the service) are compared with an existing user's template - which is generated from historical usage—by implementing a machine learning algorithm such as Random forest. The comparison result will be determined if the current user is legitimate or not. Therefore, the misuse in this paper means, any abnormal usage that is diverted from a profile while users interact with their cloud services.

The remainder of the paper is organised as follows: Sect. 2 introduces the state of the art in behavioural profiling. Section 3 presents the experimental methodology. A series of comprehensive experimental studies that evaluate the applicability of using behavioural profiling with cloud IaaS are presented in Sect. 4. Section 5 discusses the impact of the experimental results, and the conclusion and future directions of this work are presented in Sect. 6.

2 Related Work

A variety of studies have investigated behavioural profiling from a number of security perspectives, including intrusion detection, fraud detection, and authentication across different technologies (e.g. mobile phone system, network, computer system, and web browsing). Table 1 provides an analysis of these studies.

Table 1. Related behavioural profiling studies

Studies	Activity	Platform	#Participants	Performance (%)	Method	Purpose
[8]	Mobility	S	50	DR = 50, FRR = 50	Instance based learning	IDS
[9]	Telephony	S	5000	DR = 80	Genetic programing method	FD
[10]	Telephony	S	180	FRR = 3	Self-organizing map, probability	FD
[11]	Telephony	S	300	DR = 70	Neural network	FD
[12]	Mobility	S	100	DR = 81	cumulative probability and Marko properties	IDS
[13]	Mobility	S	178	DR = 94	cumulative probability and Marko properties	IDS
[14]	Telephony	S	94	DR = 97	SVM	FD
[15]	Telephony, SMS, browsing, mobility	C	50	DR = 95	Probability	Au
[16]	Telephony, SMS, browsing	C	35	EER = 1.6	Bayesian network, RBF, KNN, RF	Au
[17]	Telephony, device usage, bluetooth network scanning	C	30	EER = 13.5, 35.1, and 35.7	RBF network	Au
[18]	Application, telephony, SMS	C	76	EER = 13.5, 2.2, and 5.4	Neural network	Au
[19]	Application usage	C	76	EER = 9.8	Rule base	Au
[20]	Text, App, Web and location	C	200	EER = 3	SVM	Au
[21]	Way of using PC	C	10	EER = 7	Neural (FF-MLP)	Au
[22]	File access activity and network event	C	8	FAR = 14, FRR = 11	K-Means Clustering	Au
[23]	File access activity	C	18	FAR = 1.1	SVM	Au
[24]	Web browsing	S	100	DR = 91	support-based, lift-based profiling	I
[25]	Web browsing	S	10	EER = 24	SVM	Au

S: Server, C: Client, DR: Detection Rate, FRR: False Reject Rate, FAR: False Accept Rate, EER: Equal Error Rate, SVM: Support Vector Machine, KNN: K-Nearest Neighbours, RBF: Radial Basis Function, RF: Random Forest, FD: Fraud Detection, IDS: Intrusion Detection System, Au: Authentication, I: Identification

Early research focused mainly on IDS and fraud detection via identifying the user behaviour activities during the interaction with telephony services, such as calling and mobility [8–14]. Several classification algorithms were successfully developed to handle various attributes of defined and undefined attacks. A number of these studies implemented a large dataset (as shown in Table 1) that achieved accuracy of a Detection Rate (DR) ranging of 50% to 80%. However, the performance was not clear because the studies only show the False Rejected Rate (FRR) without including the False Accept Rate (FAR). In comparison, more recent studies focused on transparent authentication through modelling application usage to alleviate device misuse [15–20]. Much more information can be gathered from user activities while interacting with these applications (e.g. phone calls, emails, websites visits, and calendar activities). These activities were exploited to build an accurate behavioural profile which can be investigated to increase the accuracy level of the security system for the device or applications. The best accuracy result achieved in these studies were by [16] through applying four classification methods on 35 participants with an overall Equal Error Rate (EER) of 1.6%. The Random Forest classifier achieved the highest accuracy algorithm in this work with a true positive rate of 99.8% and an accuracy rate of 98.9%.

Further studies focused on the generation of user behaviour profiles from desktop computer usage to detect any illegal access to the device [21–23]. A number of features were extracted to build user behaviour profiles in the computer system, including applications being used, the time and interval of accessing files, and websites being visited. The accuracy of these studies was around 7% of EER. However, the number of participants was limited (ranging from 8 to 18 users) which does not reflect an accurate performance in practical sense. From the server side perspective, studies focused on building a user identifier by using their web surfing activities from numerous log files of websites [24, 25]. A user behaviour profiling was created based on spending time on various topics of the website, site names, number of pages, starting time and duration time of sessions. Accurate user behaviour profiles have been built to detect illegitimate usage. The best performance achieved by [24] including 100 participants with an DR of 94%. However, the study did not involve all users in the practical experiment, only a few users who had at least 300 sessions in the dataset were selected to test the system. Therefore, it is difficult to be implemented this system for solving large scale problems.

As demonstrated by existing literature, the behavioural profiling technique has been applied successfully across different technologies including mobile phones, computers (client and server) to improve the system security level. However, to the best author's knowledge, no prior work that utilises the behavioural profiling technique has been studied regarding cloud infrastructure services.

3 Experimental Methodology

The main aim of this study is to focus upon understanding to what degree behaviour profiling can be successfully applied to verify the users via their usage within cloud infrastructure services – understanding whether it is the genuine user or not in order to provide a basis for a security system to respond. Therefore, a series of experiments were conducted on a real dataset to examine the impact of a number of factors on the performance of the machine learning algorithms. These include two further research questions:

- Does the volume of data and sampling selection for training and testing have impact on performance and classification algorithms?
- How much data and time are required to generate a user template within a specific criteria?

In order to achieve these experiments, users' interactions with the cloud infrastructure application are required to be collected. However, the collection for users' activity in cloud computing services proved to be problematic. To the author's best knowledge there are no public datasets that would be used for this study; and cloud providers would be unwilling to provide such access directly due to privacy and security concerns. Whilst it is possible to create IaaS based images and have a population of participants use these machines for a specified period, it was felt this might result in behavioural patterns that do not truly reflect user's normal activities. Consequently, a decision was made to capture users' interactions within their own personal computers simulating the environment of a cloud infrastructure service. Software was developed and installed on the participants' computers. This software works in the background of the computer operating system in non-intrusive manner. Activities of 60 participants (including PhD researchers and undergraduate students) were obtained resulting in a private dataset containing 1,048,195 users' interactions. The interactions comprise the following information: the start and the end time of applications being used (e.g. Excel, Word and MatLab) and web services (URLs) being visited. The data has been anonymised to protect the participants' privacy and ethical approval was sought and obtained from the authors' institution. Table 2 demonstrates a sample of user actions within the dataset.

Table 2. User activity with personal computer

Day	Hour	Minute	Second	App/URL	Event
2	9	10	8	Word	Focus
2	9	21	16	Word	Lost focus
2	9	21	20	Endnote	Focus
2	9	23	44	Endnote	Lost focus
2	10	15	30	Paint	Focus
2	10	45	23	Paint	Lost focus
2	10	45	30	v2wLG + lIc...	Focus
2	10	49	13	v2wLG + lIc...	Lost focus

The hour, minute with applications and URLs have been used were selected as the main features set in this study which could provide a good level of pattern recognition amount the users. In order to make those features acceptable by classification algorithms, the symbolic-valued attributes (e.g. name of applications and URLs) were enumerated into numerical attributes and into the range of 0–1 [26].

The dataset of each user was divided into two sets: the first set was utilised to create a user behaviour profile for training the classification algorithm whereas the second set of the user's data was utilised to assess the performance of the algorithm (i.e. test data). Also, at no point a sample is used for both training and testing. Due to the verification nature, the data is classified into 2-class problem (i.e. either belong to legitimate users or impostors). One user acts as the genuine user, whilst all the rest users are treated as impostors. This procedure is then applied sequentially to all the other users in order to ensure they have the opportunity to represent as an authorised user. Whilst the purpose of this classification is misuse detection, the approach is determining this through verifying the authenticity of the user. As such, the results will be presented in the form of FAR, FRR and EER – standard performance metrics that are widely used in bio-metrics. The EER is widely used as a key metric to evaluate the performance (when the FAR and FRR are equal).

Two experiments were developed to investigate whether the collected data can be used to differentiate those users whom generated by. The first experiment implemented two classification algorithms on the given dataset: Random Forest (RF) and Classification And Regression Trees (CART). Decision tree algorithms are fast in identifying unknown instances in a large dataset and can easy deal with discrete attributes particularly handling outliers [27]. Therefore, the first classifier was selected due to its outstanding performance that was achieved in the previous studies (as illustrated in Table 1); while the second method was selected based on the study by [27] that conducted on different classification algorithms and the CART was a one of the best ten algorithms that achieved the highest performance. The configuration of the two selected classifiers remained as default except the number of trees of RF was modified into 30 as this number achieved a better accuracy among other configurations. Three splitting approaches for training and testing data were applied on these algorithms: 50/50, 66/34 and 80/20 in order to examine the impact of data volume on the overall performance. For each data volume setting, two sample selection methods were utilised: a random sample selection across the dataset and a time series sample selection (i.e. samples are selected sequentially as in a reality sense). The outcome of this experiment would explore how the performance of the system is affected by investigating the nature of different classification approaches. The optimal classifier can also be identified based on the findings of this experiment. Additionally, the comparison between the accuracy of the result of each data volume would give a better understanding of the nature of user behaviour profiles with the impact of the sample selection on the performance of the algorithms.

The second experiment focused upon exploring how much training data is required to generate a user template with an acceptable level of performance. For the purposes in this study an EER of 10% was set. In practice, a user profile would need to be created based upon time-series rather than random sample selection. As such, time-series sample selection was applied to achieve the goal of this experiment; the first day's data was used for training and the data from remaining days was employed for testing, then the data from first and second days was used for training and the remaining data from the rest days was utilised for testing and so on.

4   Experimental Results

4.1   Various Train/Test Set Ratio with Two Sampling Methods

The results of this experiment (as illustrated in Table 3) are encouraging to support the idea of verifying the genuine user or identifying misuse of unauthorised access to cloud infrastructure services.

As seen in Table 3, the nature of the classifier had a significant impact on improving the system performance. The CART algorithm achieved a higher accuracy than the RF method regardless the amount of data being allocated to training and testing. This includes the time series and random sample selections with the highest accuracy of 0.32% EER.

Table 3. Performance of classification algorithms

Classifier	EER (%) volume of data with time series selection			EER (%) volume of data with random selection		
	50/50	66/34	80/20	50/50	66/34	80/20
RF	15.35	13.18	12.40	4.07	3.57	3.09
CART	8.51	7.35	6.55	0.69	0.44	0.32

From the sample selection perspective, Table 3 shows that the random sample selection achieved better performance than the time series selection within both classifiers and across all volumes of training and testing data split. This can be attributed to the high probability of selecting a variety of user activities across the entire usage range whilst employing the random sample selection. It is also worth highlighting that the change in performance with both types of sample selection (random and time series) gets better as the amount of training data increases; decreases of 2% and 0.37% in EERs can be observed for time series and random selection respectively. As the proportion being reduced is significant, this suggests that the nature of user behaviour across the three-week collection period is likely to be relatively changeable. Therefore, care must be taken to ensure appropriate template renewal procedures are developed to maintain performance levels.

The classifiers' overall average performance in terms of data volume (as illustrated in Table 3) also shows that the training phase with large sample volumes achieved better performance than those with smaller data volumes. Based upon the overall average individual performance using the CART classifier with 80/20 of data splitting and random sample selection, the trend line regression approach, as illustrated in Fig. 1, also supports the same idea. Users with high volumes of interaction achieved better performance than users with fewer interactions. This support the idea put forth by prior research that more volume would provide better accuracy [17, 24, 26]. Additionally, it is logical as the classifier can learn more about the pattern usage of a user by acquiring a large volume of data, leading to better performance.

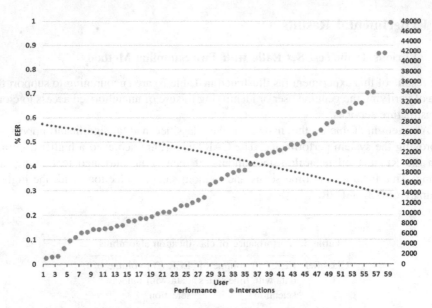

Fig. 1. Average performance based on volume of data

4.2   Time and Volume of Data Required for Generating Users Templates

This experiment focused upon the amount of data and time are required for each user to generate a user template based on predefined criteria (10% of EER). The CART classifier was chosen for this experiment due to its outstanding performance in the first experiment. In a practical sense, the data split between training the classifier and testing the performance was selected based on using the daily basis as a time window, as mentioned previously. Figure 2 demonstrates the statistical distribution (min, median, and max) of the performance of all users across 20 days.

Figure 2 shows that the classifier achieved a significantly higher performance for larger volume of training data than the low volume of samples for the training phase, specifically within the first five days. Therefore, based on the overall distribution of users' result accuracy, it suggests that at least five days of user data are needed as an overall average time to profile individuals within the given criteria. However, it can be seen on the chart that there is also a variation among actual users; some users would need less than five days and others would need more to generate the template. Therefore, further investigation is required to determine the actual time and interactions required for each user. Figure 3 demonstrates the minimum days and interactions needed for each user to build suitable user behaviour profiles.

Figure 3 shows the time and volume of interactions required to generate a user's template are different among users. For example, some users achieved the selected criteria in equal or less than two days training with lower interactions compared with other users (i.e. less than 1,500 interactions), such as users 2, 11, 32, 33, 35, and 59. In comparison, some users needed more than the half of the given period of training with high interactions (more than 17,000 interactions) to achieve the goal, such as users 40,

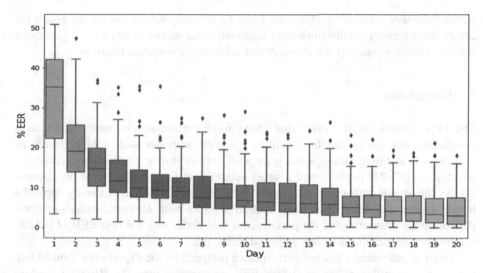

Fig. 2. Distribution of users' performance across 20 days

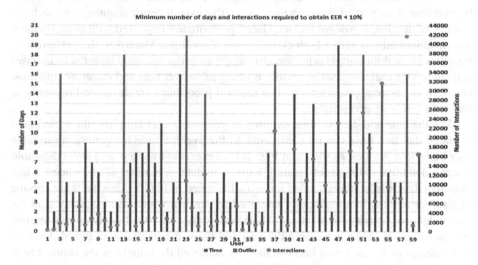

Fig. 3. Time and volume of data required for generating users' template

47, 49 and 52. Moreover, some users (outliers) did not achieve the criteria even though they had a long period of training with the highest interactions among most other users (more than 21,000 interactions) such as users 37, 51, 54, and 58. This case is a common issue for behavioural based biometrics as users' behaviour tend to change over time and under different external circumstances, which can impact negatively on the sample collection and classification performance. As less control over users and the environment exists, more care is needed when considering their implementation in a verification system. Therefore, it demonstrates that the time and volume factors worked for

80% of the user population. However, these factors may not be always necessary for determining appropriate discriminatory information for users that can help to generate a suitable temple to support the classifier for achieving the correct decision.

5 Discussion

The experimental results reveal that cloud infrastructure service users based on a simulated environment can be identified via their activities with a high degree of accuracy. In addition, although the prior work within similar environment (computer desktop) in [22–24] implemented a small dataset with limited number of participants (8-18), the overall outcome was approximately 7% of EER. While this study applied a larger dataset containing more than million samples with 60 participants—in comparison to the prior art—and the performance was better with the best EER of 0.32%, suggesting the usefulness of the proposed technique.

From an individual classifier performance perspective, the experiment showed that the CART algorithm achieved 0.32% EER and outperforms the RF with random sampling and 80/20 training and testing data splitting. This would allow other factors such as time taken to compute, computational overhead, and memory requirements to be considered as part of the selection. Also, the overall result accuracy of the large volume of data had a positive impact. Users' performance improved with more frequent activities/interactions across both classification algorithms. Moreover, the performance results with random sample selection also achieved better accuracy than the time series selection. This indicates user behaviour is changeable over time and therefore care must be taken to ensure appropriate template renewal procedures are developed regularly to maintain levels of performance.

For the time and data volume required to generate a user template, the experiment revealed that five days can be considered as the average time for generating useable user behaviour profiles, as shown in Fig. 2. However, the five days as a static threshold is not a definitive criterion for creating a user template. A number of users needed less than five days while others needed more as illustrated in Fig. 3. Also the large volume of data for training is not always guaranteed to perform with better accuracy than the low volume of activity for all users. Therefore, further statistical analysis was applied by selecting users for representing the best and worst cases. Based on Fig. 4, User 32 was selected as the best case because the user achieved the criteria in the shortest time (one day) and lowest interactions (383 interactions). User 58 was selected as the worst case as they did not achieve the criteria even though the user had the longest time (20 days) with the highest interactions (42,624 interactions). The standard deviation was calculated for the main features (time, applications and URLs) as illustrated in Fig. 4. The figure shows that User 32 had a tidy pattern of usage, which could make the classifier more able to identify the user while User 58 did not seem to have consistent usage. These changes in user behaviour can have a negative effect on the performance of classifiers because their activities are so diverse.

One reason for the worst case could be that part of the dataset was collected from early PhD research students who normally they use a variety of applications and websites during their initial research period. These variations and changes in user behaviour can affect negatively building an accurate picture of user usage pattern. Therefore, an additional mechanism is required to analyse the data deeply rather than relying on the time and volume of data alone to provide sufficient discriminatory information for creating these templates.

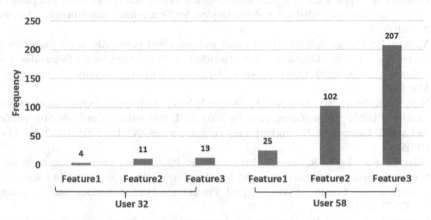

Fig. 4. Standard deviation of features' user 32 and 58

6 Conclusions

The results successfully demonstrate the ability to correctly distinguish users based on their interactions derived from a simulated cloud infrastructure service environment. Accurate user-behaviour profiles can be built to help distinguish between the normal and abnormal usage with high accuracy. Subsequently, the approach proved a highly promising solution for applying user-behavioural profiling as a supporting technique to validate users after the initial point-of-entry authentication. This can contribute and guide the system to identify a misuse of cloud services in a continuously and friendly manner.

Future work will focus on developing mechanisms for understanding the nature of the user activities traffic more deeply in order to make sure appropriate user-behaviour profiles can be generated and when and how template renewal should be undertaken.

References

1. Cisco: Cisco global cloud index: forecast and methodology, 2016–2021. White Paper (2016)
2. Abdallah, E.G., Zulkernine, M., Gu, Y.X., Liem, C.: TRUST-CAP: a trust model for cloud-based applications. In: 2017 IEEE 41st Annual Computer Software and Applications Conference (COMPSAC), vol. 2, pp. 584–589. IEEE (2017)
3. Cloud Security Alliance: The Treacherous 12 Cloud Computing Top Threats in 2016. Security, pp. 1–34 (2016)

4. Chen, D., Zhao, H.: Data security and privacy protection issues in cloud computing. In: 2012 International Conference Computer Science and Electronics Engineering, vol. 1, pp. 647–651 (2012)
5. Walters, R.: Cyber attacks on U.S. companies in 2016. The Heritage Foundation: Issue Brief No. 4636 (2016)
6. Cameron, D.: Apple knew of iCloud security hole 6 months before Celebgate. The Daily Dot (2014). https://www.dailydot.com/debug/apple-icloud-brute-force-attack-march/. Accessed 27 Feb 2018
7. Yadron, D.: Hacker collects 272 m email addresses and passwords, some from Gmail | Technology | The Guardian. The Guardian (2016). https://www.theguardian.com/technology/2016/may/04/gmail-yahoo-email-password-hack-hold-security. Accessed 10 Mar 2018
8. Hall, J., Barbeau, M., Kranakis, E.: Anomaly-based intrusion detection using mobility profiles of public transportation users. In: 2005 IEEE International Conference on Wireless and Mobile Computing, Networking and Communications, WiMob 2005, vol. 2, pp. 17–24 (2005)
9. Hilas, C., Kazarlis, S., Rekanos, I., Mastorocostas, P.: A genetic programming approach to telecommunications fraud detection and classification. In: Proceedings of 2014 International Conference on Circuits, System Signal Processing, Communications and Computers, pp. 77–83 (2014)
10. Ogwueleka, F.: Fraud detection in mobile communications networks using user profiling and classification techniques. J. Sci. Technol. 29, 31–42 (2009)
11. Qayyum, S., Mansoor, S., Khalid, A., Halim, Z., Baig, A.R.: Fraudulent call detection for mobile networks. In: 2010 International Conference on Information Emerging Technologies, pp. 1–5 (2010). https://doi.org/10.1109/iciet.2010.5625718
12. Yazji, S., Dick, R.P., Scheuermann, P., Trajcevski, G.: Protecting private data on mobile systems based on spatio-temporal analysis (2011)
13. Yazji, S., Scheuermann, P., Dick, R.P., Trajcevski, G., Jin, R.: Efficient location aware intrusion detection to protect mobile devices. Pers. Ubiquitous Comput. 18, 143–162 (2014)
14. Subudhi, S., Panigrahi, S.: Quarter-sphere support vector machine for fraud detection in mobile telecommunication networks. Procedia Comput. Sci. 48, 353–359 (2015)
15. Shi, E., Niu, Y., Jakobsson, M., Chow, R.: Implicit authentication through learning user behavior. In: Burmester, M., Tsudik, G., Magliveras, S., Ilić, I. (eds.) Information Security, vol. 6531, pp. 99–113. Springer, Heidelberg (2011). https://doi.org/10.1007/978-3-642-18178-8_9
16. Damopoulos, D., Menesidou, S.A., Kambourakis, G., Papadaki, M., Gritzalis, S., Clarke, N.: Evaluation of anomaly-based IDS for mobile devices using machine learning classifiers. Secur. Commun. Netw. 5, 3–14 (2012)
17. Li, F., Clarke, N., Papadaki, M., Dowland, P.: Behaviour profiling on mobile devices. In: Proceedings of - EST 2010 - 2010 International Conference on Emerging Security Technologies, pp. 77–82 (2010). ROBOSEC 2010 - Robots and Security. LAB-RS 2010 - Learning and Adaptive Behavior in Robotic Systems
18. Li, F., Clarke, N., Papadaki, M., Dowland, P.: Misuse detection for mobile devices using behaviour profiling. Int. J. Cyber Warf. Terror. 1, 41–53 (2011)
19. Li, F., Clarke, N., Papadaki, M., Dowland, P.: Active authentication for mobile devices utilising behaviour profiling. Int. J. Inf. Secur. 13, 229–244 (2014)
20. Fridman, L., Weber, S., Greenstadt, R., Kam, M.: Active authentication on mobile devices via stylometry, application usage, web browsing, and GPS location. IEEE Syst. J. 11, 513–521 (2017)

21. Aupy, A., Clarke, N.: User authentication by service utilisation profiling. Adv. Netw. Commun. Eng. **2**, 18 (2005). School of Computing, Communications & Electronics, University of Plymouth
22. Yazji, S., Chen, X., Dick, R.P., Scheuermann, P.: Implicit user re-authentication for mobile devices. In: Zhang, D., Portmann, M., Tan, A.H., Indulska, J. (eds.) Ubiquitous Intelligence and Computing, vol. 5585, pp. 325–339. Springer, Heidelberg (2009). https://doi.org/10.1007/978-3-642-02830-4_25
23. Salem, M.B., Stolfo, S.J.: Modeling user search behavior for masquerade detection. In: Sommer, R., Balzarotti, D., Maier, G. (eds.) Recent Advances in Intrusion Detection, vol. 6961, pp. 181–200. Springer, Heidelberg (2011). https://doi.org/10.1007/978-3-642-23644-0_10
24. Yang, Y.: Web user behavioral profiling for user identification. Decis. Support Syst. **49**, 261–271 (2010)
25. Abramson, M., Aha, D.: User authentication from web browsing behavior. In: Twenty-Sixth International FLAIRS Conference, pp, 268–273 (2013)
26. Sola, J., Sevilla, J.: Importance of input data normalization for the application of neural networks to complex industrial problems. IEEE Trans. Nucl. Sci. **44**, 1464–1468 (1997)
27. Wu, X., et al.: Top 10 algorithms in data mining. Knowl. Inf. Syst. **14**, 1–37 (2008)

Dissuading Stolen Password Reuse

Slim Trabelsi[1(✉)] and Chedy Missaoui[2(✉)]

[1] SAP Security Research, 805, Avenue Dr. M. Donat, Mougins, France
slim.trabelsi@sap.com
[2] Tessan Group, Rue des Jardins, Tunis, Tunisia
chedy.missaoui@gmail.com

Abstract. The whole security community agreed on the fact that login and password based authentication systems are one of the weakest point of the current systems. Despite this global consensus password based credentials are still the most used identification and authentication method used on internet. One of the main reason for this weakness is due to the password leak phenomena. For several reasons (described in this paper) password databases are frequently leaked and shared publicly. Once these passwords it will be very hard for a user to protect his digital life, especially if this password is used in several websites (what we call domino effect). In this paper we propose a solution to reduce the attempts for replaying stolen passwords. We measure the efficiency of this solution via a deployment and the analysis on a fake website exposed to a fake password leak.

Keywords: Passwords · Leakage · Hacking · Cyber security · Authentication

1 Introduction

Bruce Schneider said: "As insecure as passwords generally are, they're not going away anytime soon. Every year you have more and more passwords to deal with, and every year they get easier and easier to break.". Despite that fact, password authentication systems are still dominating the authentication landscape especially on internet websites (less inside big companies where certificate-based authentication is becoming more and more popular [10]). Many technological and cultural reasons are explaining this phenomenon [11] and this issue will stay for several years in the future. According to The Breach Level Index [1] every day more than 5 million records are stolen and only 4% are encrypted. The rest is in clear text or hashed and finally easily accessible to cyber criminals. A Large portion of this data is composed of credentials and all the content is at some point of time published for free on internet. One of the recent biggest clear text credentials disclosure was recently released [2], with more than 1.4 Billion entries compiled from several leaks. Almost all the big internet companies suffered at some point of time from a credential leak (Apple, Amazon [3], LinkedIn [4], Twitter [5], Microsoft [6]), and according to a recent study [7] 65% of data beaches result from weak or stolen passwords. And without being paranoid we are almost all concerned by a password leak at some point of time in our digital life. In some of the cases we are not even aware about the theft.

One password leak could have much more disease that expected, and this is due to the password replication custom from certain people to use the same password for many domains or a derivation a root password easy to guess. For example, if your Gmail account was leaked, a malicious user would try to replay it for Hotmail, Yahoo, LinkedIn, Facebook, Twitter or even your professional e-mail account. If the password is the same everywhere the whole digital life of a person can be ruined. This phenomenon is called domino effect [8]. The Mozilla bug tracker (Bugzilla) was severely hacked in 2014 due to a domino effect affecting one of their administrator who was using the same password Bugzilla management and his twitter account [9]. His Twitter password was leaked, and the hackers replay it on Mozilla. The result of this hack was the full access to all security notes including zero-day vulnerabilities, exploit code related to all Mozilla software. All the security experts were recommending to not use Firefox until all the security breaches are fixed. The domino effect is not only concerning basic password reuse, but it concerns password reshape. Due to the human limitation of memorizing various combinations of passwords related to all their online accounts, one option is to create passwords starting from a common root word. Like example a root password is *ILikefootball* and the derivations will be {*ILikefootball1234, ILikefootball&"'$$, footballILike9871*, etc.}. Some algorithms [12] can guess those types of variations and make the domino effect much more harmful.

For this reason, in this paper we propose a solution to try to discourage hackers to reuse stolen passwords to compromise users accounts. We measure the impact of this solution by deploying a fake banking website and leaking fake credentials. We observe then the reaction of the hackers when the dissuasion process is triggered.

This paper is organized as follows: in Sect. 2 we describe the different reasons and factors that leads to a password leak. In Sect. 3 we list the different channels used to spread stolen credentials. In Sect. 4 we describe our honeypot case study. In Sect. 5 we introduce our solution to dissuade the stolen password reuse, and we evaluate the impact of this solution on our honeypot. In Sect. 6 we declare our ethical considerations applied to conduct this study. In Sect. 7 we describe our state of the art study, then we conclude.

2 How Credentials Are Leaked

There is a multitude of reasons at the origin of a password leak. In this section, we give a non-exhaustive list of methods and attacks used by attackers to obtain credentials from websites, systems and people.

2.1 Vulnerability Exploit

The software vulnerability is defined as a weakness of a failure existing in the source code of the system that can be exploited by an attacker to perform malicious actions. Exploiting such vulnerability can require writing a code or execute a work-flow process in a different way from what it was initially designed. An SQL injection attack is for example exploiting a bad input validation vulnerability and can lead to the entire database dump including the password tables.

To exploit vulnerabilities cyber criminals, had the good idea to make script kiddie's life easier by developing easy to use and automated tools called exploit kits. These tools will target a system make an analysis, identify all the potential vulnerabilities and execute the related exploit attack. This kind of tools contributed to the democratization [13] of micro-bloggings attacks and resulted of many data breaches, including credential dumps.

2.2 Social Engineering and Phishing

The social engineering attacks, is based on the exploitation of human trust to extract confidential information from a victim. It is based on a psychological manipulation that masquerades an entity of trust to the victim in order to ask for personal or confidential information. One of the most known method of this attack in information security is called Phishing attack. A phishing attack is mainly spread though e-mails, it takes the appearance of a professional or serious e-mail (management, bank, support team, etc.) but it redirects to a pitfall. For a massive Phishing attacks, Phishing kits are available to automate the fake e-mail distribution, the deployment of trap servers and the collection of credentials.

2.3 Keyloggers and Malwares

Some malwares are exploiting vulnerabilities of the systems to access their databases or file set, some others install keyloggers to capture all the keyboard entries of the victim. Credentials are then collected and sent through the network to the attacker servers. Even if most of the antiviruses can detect traditional keyloggers, some malicious browsers plugins remain undetected and continue to steal keyboard typing. Other types of malware are used to intercept system and configuration files to identify credentials.

2.4 Easy to Guess and Default Passwords

In all the best practice recommendations related to the password setup, the rule number one is to not chose an easy password. This rule is elementary event if some persons are still ignoring it. This issue becomes really dramatic when system administrators are committing the error in wide scale. We can refer to a practice that was spread among hardware vendors to set default passwords[1] for systems (usually the same one). Big industrial companies were targeted by attackers exploiting[2] the default password vulnerability. Or in some other cases system administrators chose to use personal identifiers of the users to create passwords like birthdate or social security numbers, etc. This would open the floor to easy guessing attacks like the Yale vs Princeton case.

---

[1] https://www.scmagazine.com/russian-researchers-leak-default-passwords-packaged-to-icsscada-software/article/527829/.

[2] https://www.nytimes.com/2002/07/26/nyregion/princeton-pries-into-web-site-for-yale-applicants.html.

2.5   Honeypots and Traps

Cyber criminals are permanently inventing new strategies to collect people credentials, some of them are elaborated and require a long-term effort. In some cases, they create real websites and services like discussion forums, adult websites, storage platforms or free virtual machines. These platforms are of course collecting all the credentials created by their users and rely on the domino effect [8] to compromise other accounts from their users. Even if some studies pointed out this phenomenon [14] very few statistics are available to quantify the impact of such sophisticated attacks.

3   Where Credentials Are Published

There are several sources sharing stolen credentials. Depending on the freshness and the quality of the data, these sources can be paying or free.

3.1   Commercial Sources

One of the main motivation to leak data and more specifically credential is the financial gain that could be generated from this action. We observe frequently cyber criminals selling credentials on the black markets in the dark web marketplaces. The prices and the popularity can vary with the freshness and the sensitivity of the data sold. In 2016[3] for example a hacker was selling a bunch of US government credentials in the dark web for very high prices. In this case the credentials sold are very sensitive, rare and fresh. Then a chain of resellers will appear in order to invest in this kind of merchandize and create mini-websites to sell the credentials per entry or per package of 10. This kind of stolen credential will be cascaded through several sub-sources until becoming free at some point of time. There is a real illegal business in the password resell. Without being a talented hacker, a simple reseller can generate a lot of money just by collecting and reselling credentials. A lot of people were arrested[4] for running such kind of credential reselling business.

3.2   Free Sources

In the previous section, we exhaustively described the leaked password lifecycle in the illegal commercial circuit that ends-up in to a free sharing platform. According to most of the recent studies, text sharing websites like PasteBin are the most commonly used platforms to share free stolen credential or to advertise on sales by sharing part of the stolen databases. Hacking forums like hackforums.net, offensivecommunity.net, or bestblackhatforums.eu, are also popular places to share this kind of data, even if the access is restricted (needs account creation and works with a credit compensation

---

[3] http://www.businessinsider.fr/us/hacker-selling-credentials-government-sites-2016-7.
[4] https://thehackernews.com/2018/01/leakedsource-operator-charged.html.

system based on the contribution). Some torrent hosts are also used to share huge databases. These sources are easily accessible by most of the users on internet and offers a huge collection of stolen passwords that is maintained and enriched over the time.

Some legal websites are also offering the possibility to check whether their credentials were leaked at some point of time. Websites like have I been pwned[5] gives the possibility to provide your login or password and find how many times they were leaked. They also offer commercial services to sell the data per domain or to alert when a credential is leaked. This kind of websites are collecting the publicly available leaked databases. Some discussions are still ongoing on the morality of making legal business by offering services based on stolen passwords.

4 Dissuading Stolen Password Reuse

In this paper, we propose a new solution to deter and prevent malicious people from reusing stolen or hacked credentials to illegally access users accounts. We put in place a system that will threaten the authors of this illegal access tentative exploiting the stolen credentials.

4.1 Concept

When a website or a domain is hacked, the administrator is at some point of time notified about the issue. The administrator of hacked website will then put in place a password change process to all their users by notifying them and asking to change password (ideally using two factor authentication). Once this step done, the administrator will observe the account updates from the user. Once a login tentative using the old stolen credential is detected, the attacker will be redirected to a honeypot version of the website. He will be invited to perform an account 'recovery' process (that seem very legitimate to the attacker). At this step the same system used in our honeypot can be used by the domain host.

During this process (described in Fig. 2), the attacker will be asked to provide information to recover the blocked user account such as: email address, (second recovery email address), phone number and a new password. He will be then asked to confirm all this information by sending a verification email, an SMS code or a phone call. At the same time, all the attacker's navigation metadata will be collected: IP address, browser fingerprint (user agent, list of installed plugins, language, screen size, Operating system etc. ...), VPN provider and address if used, Internet Service Provider, IP Geolocation. We also inject tracking cookies and we create a virtual profile of the attacker. We might also try to scan his IP address to detect open ports, and detect running applications.

---

[5] https://haveibeenpwned.com/.

When the attacker reaches the state "Warning" in Fig. 3, the honeypot will display a warning message containing all his data and explaining that he is in a law infringement that could lead him to court judgement (see the warning message displayed Fig. 1). The machine signature is then blacklisted in order to block any other tentative.

Fig. 1. Violation warning message

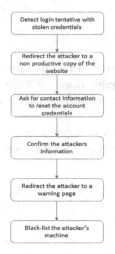

Fig. 2. Dissuading password reuse process

Fig. 3. Honeypot website capture

5   Experiments, Measurements and Validation

The goal of this study is to try to identify the profile of the persons that are illegally re-using leaked passwords shared on internet. We try to capture their behaviour and their anonymity degree. We also propose a counter-measure to reduce the re-usage motivation of the attacker.

5.1   Honeypot Bank Website

We decided to create a fake website of middle eastern bank. We also generated fake credentials dataset (containing Arabic names as logins). We choose Middle Est due to the convergence of several studies identifying their banks as the most targeted ones by the various attackers.

   We generated 3300 credentials distributed over 10 well known websites for credentials sharing on the surface web and the dark web. Here are the links to the sites:

- https://pastebin.com
- https://www.pastefs.com
- https://slexy.org/recent
- http://n0z.de/index.php
- https://pastie.ru
- https://justpaste.it
- https://pastelink.net/read
- https://ideone.com/recent
- http://nzxj65x32vh2fkhk.onion (Stronghold)
- http://depastedihrn3jtw.onion

We started the experience on March 2nd 2018 and we recorded for a duration of three weeks. We made 11 rounds of distribution to these sites (until March 11th), to ensure a good visibility. For every site, we publish a specific set of credentials to easily identify the site origin of the interaction.

Architecture

The Honeypot system was deployed on a cloud hosting service with a decoupled system backup to save data in case of attack (see Fig. 4).

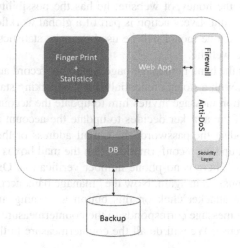

Fig. 4. Honeypot architecture

The Web application is exposing the web interface (Fig. 3) and implementing the workflow of the user interaction including the deception system put in place (will be described further in this paper). As mentioned previously, in order to protect our system and the data collected we put in place a firewall system and an anti-DoS attack framework. This security system is intercepting all the incoming requests to the web app. All the interactions and the credentials are persisted in a local DB that is also connected to the fingerprint and the analysis engine. This component is charge of collecting the navigation information and the traces left by the users while they are accessing the website. The statistics engine is in charge of the analysis and the computing of all the events and the interactions happening in the system in order to facilitate our study.

Fingerprint

A browser fingerprint is the combination of several identification parameters that will make the browser uniquely identifiable. The browser fingerprint can be quantified into a signature calculated by the combination of numerical values associated to the different parameters. In our study we choose of the following parameters to compute the signature: Browser Type, Browser version, Browser name, Operating system, Is Beta, Is Crawler, is Win16, Is Win32, Supports frames, Supports tables, Supports Cookies,

Supports VB Scripts, Supports JavaScript, JavaScript version, Supports Java Applets, Supports ActiveX Controls, User IP Address, User Host name, Remote port, Country, Language, Plugins, Time-zone.

All these elements combined will generate a signature used to identify distinct users running traditional browsers. In order to compute this signature, we create a matrix with all these parameters and for every new entry we increment a numerical value. The union of these values will generate a signature vector.

State Machine

When a user accesses the honeypot website, he has the possibility to execute certain actions in the bank account. Every action is part of a global workflow that we depicted in Fig. 5. This state machine model will be used to make statistics on the behavior of every user visiting the website.

When a user visits the bank homepage page we do not record any trace (not useful). When the user logs-in with a stolen credential then the tracking starts. Once the user is logged in, an information message invites him to update the account password and the contact information. If the attacker decides to update the account information, he will have the choice to update the password, the e-mail address or the phone number. In case of e-mail address update, a conformation from the mail box is needed to check the validity of the address. There is no phone number verification. Once this information updated the attacker must login again. Now the "manage bank account" button appears in the interface, if the attacker click on this button a warning message is displayed (Fig. 1). This warning message corresponds to the countermeasure put in place to limit the stolen credential reuse. We will detail the countermeasure in the following section of the paper.

5.2   Observations

The credentials were published for 15 days. We are aware that most of the experimented hackers will first verify the presence of the Bank on internet before any interaction with the website. For this reason, we suppose that most of the users are curious and intermediary and beginner's gold diggers.

We recorded in total 741 interactions (we define an interaction as an evolution in each step of the interaction workflow described in Fig. 5). These interactions are made by three categories of users: TOR protected users, Proxy protected users and non-protected users (accessing via private and public internet connections). 449 interactions are done by non-protected users; this represents more than 60% of the total interactions. 51 interactions by TOR users 6% and the rest 244 using web proxies 33% (Fig. 6).

Users using a web or a TOR proxy don't have a unique browsing finger print; those kinds of proxies are usually sharing fake browsing information in order to anonymize users and make their finger print not unique. For the non-protected users we identified 88 unique signatures (this probably corresponds to 88 unique users). On these unique signatures we were able to locate the IP addresses per country.

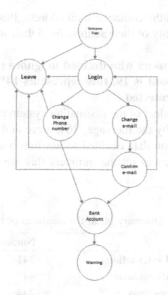

Fig. 5. Honeypot interaction state machine

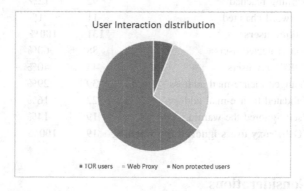

Fig. 6. User interaction distribution per browsing mode

5.3 Measurements and Results

Based on several parameters that we identified (date, time, selected user account, new password set) we guess that 43 unique users were navigating using a proxy or TOR. This number is not totally exact due to the difficulty to identify unique signatures. This raises the number of total unique users to 131.

On 741 interactions, the warning was reached 92 times 12%. As a reminder, according to Fig. 3, the warning is reached when the attacker decided to access the victim's account (after changing the password or not). The password was changed only 11 times. This represents only 1% of the interaction, this is an indication on the need for the attacker to leave the user account as it is and not raise any suspicion.

39 unique users changed the contact e-mail address, this represent 29% of the total users. 22 confirmed the validity of their address from their mail box, this represent 16% of the users.

The number of unique users who decided to ignore the warning and try again to access to the bank account is 19, this represents 14% of the whole users and they are all proxy/TOR protected.

We clearly observe the effect of the dissuading system put in place. Even if 14% of the users were not threaten by the message, 86% were and all the non-protected users who observed their navigation data decided to not follow-up on the illegal activity.

The table below summarizes all the numbers that we collected during the study (Table 1).

Table 1. Summary of all the measures of the study

Data	Number	Proportion
Total recorded interactions	**741**	**100%**
Non-protected interactions	449	60%
Web proxy interactions	244	33%
TOR interactions	51	7%
Warning reached	92	12%
Password changed	11	1%
Unique users	**131**	**100%**
Non-protected users	88	60%
TOR/Proxy users	43	40%
Changed their e-mail address	39	29%
Validated their e-mail address	22	16%
Users ignored the warning	19	14%
TOR/Proxy users ignored the warning	**19**	**100%**

6   Ethical Considerations

The honeypot deployed and the honey tokens distributed are completely fake and non-exploitable by attackers. The bank is a fake one, the services are fake and the names used for the logins are generated randomly. The data collected is only used for research purpose. All the data is deleted just after the study with a retention period of one month. The users that connected to the honeypot are not identified and their data is never crossed or combined with other datasets for identification purposes. The server used in the experiments was running only with patched software to reduce the exposure risk. We used different protection tools (anti-dos, firewall, input sanitizing, etc.). During all the experiment period, we checked permanently the logs of our systems in order to detect external access. Zero abnormal access detected. All these precautions were taken in order to avoid an external attack and an eventual collection of data.

7 Related Work

Most of the solutions proposed in the literature suggest bypassing the multiplication of password versions by adopting complex centralized infrastructures for authentication [17] and [18]. Multifactor authentication [16] and other hardware devices based solutions are popular in the literature but some of them are bypassed and they are not designed to dissuade hackers to reuse stolen passwords. Several studies were conducted to define and explain the domino effect phenomena due to the password reuse bad practice of the users [8]. Other studies explored the different password guessing techniques used from stolen credential databases [12]. These techniques are used to generate variants of a password root. These variants are frequently adopted by the users to vary their password collection set among the different domains and websites.

A Google study [15] proposed the first longitudinal measurement research tracking the origin of the different credential leak sources and their impact on user account (in term of re-use rate). This study tackles the origin of the leak and not the consequences and who is behind these consequences. The proposed mitigation techniques are based on two factor authentications.

8 Discussion and Conclusion

In this paper we proposed a new process dissuading hackers and malicious users to reuse stolen passwords to access illegally users accounts. In order to validate this solution, we created a fake banking website and spread 3300 fake credentials. We observed the behaviour of the users re-using these credentials and identified the different categories of hacker profiles. The results of our study give an idea on the type of users re-using stolen credentials, their degree of security precautions taken to perform illegal actions, and the impact of our dissuading warning-based message. One important observation, is that all the users who are not surfing behind an anonymous proxy are threaten by our prevention system especially when their navigation information are displayed. Concerning the other more precautious users only 19% ignored the system. This ratio is quite interesting according to our opinion and reflects the fear of being tracked by this category of users, that we promptly describe as vultures that want to dig some gold from crumbs resulting of big hacks.

In the literature we can find some complex solutions [19] to identify TOR proxy users, solutions that we cannot implement on a research lab level. Some other approaches [15] suggest using malwares to track hackers activities, but this approach can have legal issues.

In our future work, we want to explore new methods to collect useful information from TOR or proxy users in order to enhance the efficiency of our dissuasion system and reduce the password replay tentative.

Acknowledgement. This work was partly supported by EU-funded H2020 project C3ISP [grand no. 700294].

References

1. http://breachlevelindex.com/
2. Database of 1.4 Billion Credentials Found on Dark Web. https://www.securityweek.com/database-14-billion-credentials-found-dark-web
3. How APPLE and AMAZON Security Flaws Led to My Epic Hacking. https://www.wired.com/2012/08/apple-amazon-mat-honan-hacking/
4. LinkedIn Lost 167 Million Account Credentials in Data Breach. http://fortune.com/2016/05/18/linkedin-data-breach-email-password/
5. Passwords for 32M Twitter accounts may have been hacked and leaked. https://techcrunch.com/2016/06/08/twitter-hack/
6. Password Leak Lists Contain 20 Percent of Microsoft Login Credentials. https://www.forbes.com/sites/adriankingsleyhughes/2012/07/16/hackers-have-20-percent-of-microsoft-login-credentials/#54cb833c7e0d
7. 63% of Data Breaches Result from Weak or Stolen Passwords. http://info.idagent.com/blog/63-of-data-breaches-result-from-weak-or-stolen-passwords
8. Ives, B., Walsh, K.R., Schneider, H.: The domino effect of password reuse. Commun. ACM 47(4), 75–78 (2004). https://doi.org/10.1145/975817.975820
9. Mozilla: data stolen from hacked bug database was used to attack Firefox. https://arstechnica.com/information-technology/2015/09/mozilla-data-stolen-from-hacked-bug-database-was-used-to-attack-firefox/?utm_content=buffer1c53c&utm_medium=social&utm_source=twitter.com&utm_campaign=buffer
10. 2017 state of authentication report. https://fidoalliance.org/wp-content/uploads/The-State-of-Authentication-Report.pdf
11. Herley, C., Van Oorschot, P.: A research agenda acknowledging the persistence of passwords. IEEE Secur. Priv. 10(1), 28–36 (2012). https://doi.org/10.1109/msp.2011.150
12. Das, A., Bonneau, J., Caesar, M., Borisov, N., Wang, X.: The tangled web of password reuse. In: NDSS, vol. 14, pp. 23–26, February 2014
13. Akiyama, M., Yagi, T., Aoki, K., Hariu, T., Kadobayashi, Y.: Active credential leakage for observing web-based attack cycle. In: Stolfo, S.J., Stavrou, A., Wright, C.V. (eds.) RAID 2013. LNCS, vol. 8145, pp. 223–243. Springer, Heidelberg (2013). https://doi.org/10.1007/978-3-642-41284-4_12
14. Claycomb, W.R., Nicoll, A.: Insider threats to cloud computing: directions for new research challenges. In: 2012 IEEE 36th Annual Computer Software and Applications Conference (COMPSAC), pp. 387–394. IEEE (2012)
15. Thomas, K., et al.: Data breaches, phishing, or malware?: understanding the risks of stolen credentials. In: Proceedings of the 2017 ACM SIGSAC Conference on Computer and Communications Security, pp. 1421–1434. ACM, October 2017
16. Dasgupta, D., Roy, A., Nag, A.: Multi-factor authentication. In: Dasgupta, D., Roy, A., Nag, A. (eds.) Advances in User Authentication. Springer, Cham, 185–233 (2017). https://doi.org/10.1007/978-3-319-58808-7_5
17. Sun, H.M., Chen, Y.H., Lin, Y.H.: oPass: a user authentication protocol resistant to password stealing and password reuse attacks. IEEE Trans. Inf. Forensics Secur. 7(2), 651–663 (2012)
18. Kontaxis, G., Athanasopoulos, E., Portokalidis, G., Keromytis, A.D.: SAuth: protecting user accounts from password database leaks. In: Proceedings of the 2013 ACM SIGSAC Conference on Computer & Communications Security, pp. 187–198. ACM, November 2013
19. Schneier, B.: Attacking tor: how the NSA targets users' online anonymity. The Guardian, vol. 4 (2013)

Author Index

Printed in the United States
By Bookmasters